THEY SAW
AMERICA FIRST

By KATHERINE and
JOHN BAKELESS

Illustrated

In 1492 the continent of North America was a rich wilderness. Animals, birds and fish existed in abundance impossible for us to imagine today. The forests filled the air with the scent of many flowers. Fruit, nuts and other edible plants were more than sufficient for the small number of Indians who were scattered over the land. This was what the explorers found, but few realized the extent of the wealth they saw. The hunt for gold drew them on through unbelievable hardships, heedless of the riches at hand.

The authors of this book have shown us how the New World looked to these adventurers. We follow the journeys of the explorers from Columbus to Lewis and Clark and learn of the courage, cruelty, greed and imagination that possessed the men who opened up to Europeans the great continent on which we live.

This volume is illustrated with old woodcuts and paintings. It has a clear map which shows the journeys of the various explorers and an index. Mr. Bakeless' distinguished *The Eyes of Discovery*, now out of print, was the basis for this new book on American exploration.

THEY SAW
AMERICA
FIRST

THEY SAW

Our First Explorers
and What They Saw

Philadelphia • New York

AMERICA FIRST

By Katherine and
John Bakeless

J. B. Lippincott Company

CONTENTS

Books by Katherine Bakeless

IN THE BIG TIME
STORY-LIVES OF GREAT COMPOSERS
STORY-LIVES OF AMERICAN COMPOSERS

Books by John Bakeless

BACKGROUND TO GLORY: The Life of George Rogers Clark
THE EYES OF DISCOVERY: America As Seen by the First Explorers

LIST OF ILLUSTRATIONS

(In this order following page 126)

Map drawing follows page 13

THEY SAW
AMERICA
FIRST

1492

I
T WAS midnight of October 11-12 and the whole course of world history was going to change forever, in just two hours more.

No one in the whole world knew it. No one even guessed. Nobody, at that historic moment, could grasp the stupendous idea of what was happening. But every man in the little fleet of three small ships, from the admiral down to the youngest page boy, was tensely alert. They could feel that *something* was going to happen. They could not even guess how tremendous it was going to be.

There was a reward of money for the man who first sighted land; and everyone knew, by this time, that the long voyage was nearly over. Sometime, soon, something was going to come up over that western horizon, where for so long eager eyes had seen nothing but waves and more waves, endlessly tossing.

As midnight approached, the three little sailing ships were scudding ahead, as fast as they could go, through a clear, moon-and-starlit night. Luckily, they had a following wind. The moon, past full, was riding high, behind them. That was another fortunate chance. The moon happened to be in the one best position to shine on whatever lay ahead, in the mysterious, unknown sea to westward, which no white man's eye had ever seen and to which all eyes on the three ships were straining now.

Nerves were tense in all three crews. For more than a month they had been at sea, sailing always west, until the chance that any of them would ever live to return at all seemed well-nigh impossible. Never anything on the horizon but the eternal ocean, and more of it than they—or any human being then—had ever dreamed could possibly exist.

There was good reason why nerves were tense. These three ships, bearing about ninety men in all (including some page boys, ship's boys, and servants) were the first that had ever attempted to cross the vast expanse of salt water, which, at home in Spain, was called the "Ocean Sea." It was a wholly unknown sea, and the unknown is a fearful thing, even to the bravest.

Two long weeks earlier, Martín Alonzo Pinzón, captain of the *Pinta,* had thought he saw land. But the captain had been wrong. They were then almost exactly in the middle of the Atlantic, with no land for more than a thousand miles. Once more, on October 9, *Niña* had been so sure land was in sight that she joyfully ran up her flag and fired a signal gun. Wrong again!

It was the birds that really set Christopher Columbus on the right course. October is the great migration month, in that North America toward which three ships were headed. It was a forested land that had in it, then, more birds than it would ever have again. The adventurers had chanced upon the season when feathered millions fly south, some of them—like the swallows—plunging across the Gulf of Mexico, for South America, while others go down the coast, across Bermuda, to the West Indies. The ancestors of the birds we know were doing the same thing in October, five hundred years ago.

It was a flock of the latter group of migrants that caught the anxious eye of the great explorer. Where birds are flying, there must be land. Columbus altered his course to follow them. Two nights later, the crews could hear more birds, calling overhead in the darkness, and occasionally could see them against the brilliant tropical moon.

In spite of such encouraging signs, there was mutiny aboard *Santa María* next day. The sailors were afraid. It had been a long time since they had seen land. The men were losing nerve. Worse still, they were getting on each other's nerves.

The little expedition had sailed out of the harbor of Palos, Spain, on Friday, August 3, 1492, heading for the Canary Islands. They had to delay there for repairs. *Pinta* had damaged her rudder. After leaving the Canaries on September 6, they had seen nothing since but water, water, and still more water. To the ignorant seamen, it seemed high time to turn back. They had not spent years in planning this amazing voyage, as had their leader. Nor did these simple sailors share the powerful belief in one idea that fired the mind of Christopher Columbus.

They began to think it was all just a fancy of their leader's. The "Ocean Sea" was proving bigger than anyone had ever imagined. Their ships seemed very small in such a wide world of waves. Weary of stale food, stale water, and the monotonous diet of salt meat, dried peas, and hard "biscuit" day after day, any eagerness they may have felt at first had turned to cold fear. There was no tingle of adventure in their voyage now. They saw only monotony and danger. They could not grasp the idea that they were sailing on the greatest adventure of all time, under the boldest explorer of all ages.

There was only one way for Columbus to quell the mutiny. He took it. He promised to turn back, unless they struck land in three more days. No wonder his three ships were sailing fast on that October night. Even when the wind approached gale strength, Columbus refused to take in sail. His time was running out. He *had* to make a landfall.

Soon it began to look as if three days would be enough. Encouraging signs of land began to appear. Some one on *Niña* fished a branch bearing small blossoms out of the water. *Pinta* caught up, from the sea, a cane, a stick, a piece of board, a plant that obviously had grown on land, and finally, a second stick that appeared to have been carved or shaped with a tool. After these signs, the grumbling stopped. Everybody now felt sure they were approaching land at last.

On the evening of October 11, after the sailors on the *Santa María*

had sung their evening hymn, Columbus made an impressive speech to his crew. He thought it probable that they would sight land that very night. There must be vigilant lookout. He promised a doublet of velvet—in addition to the prize money—to the first man who saw land. At sunset, he changed course again, this time, straight to the west.

Though Columbus did not know it, those two changes—first when he turned west-south-west to follow the migrating birds, second when he turned straight west again, on the evening of October 11, were very fortunate. He and all his men probably owed their lives to the birds' passing overhead, just at the right time. If he had not followed those flocks, he would have sailed into the Gulf Stream. He would not have been prepared for its powerful current. No one knew there was such a thing, in those days. The voyagers would have landed on the North American coast—if they had landed at all. But the chances are they would have been wrecked in Florida, then unknown, where many a sailor left his bones in the years that followed.

If Columbus had failed to make that second change in his course— westward again—he would have brought up somewhere south of San Salvador, on an unfriendly island shore, in a very dangerous situation. Luck and the migrating birds brought him safely to the southern end of an island called Guanahané, which Columbus renamed San Salvador, in honor of the Holy Saviour, on whose protection he had relied.

The captains of the three ships had taken turns leading the fleet. On that night of destiny, Captain Martín Alonzo Pinzón, on *Pinta,* was in the lead. *Pinta* was the fastest sailing ship of the three. Columbus himself was on the flagship, *Santa María,* the largest. (The little *Niña* was Columbus's favorite, and he was to return aboard her.)

At ten o'clock that Thursday night, just before the moon rose, Columbus—anxiously pacing his quarter-deck—thought he saw a light. One other man, straining his eyes, too, also believed he saw a faint flicker. Then Columbus thought he saw it again, "like a little wax candle rising and falling." Still another seaman thought he saw it and called out, "Lumbre! Tierra!" Light! Land! But Columbus's young page said to him, haughtily, "It's already seen by my master." Some "saw" it, but most did not. Many writers have tried to explain what that mysterious light may possibly have been. It may have been a star, so close to the horizon that the waves blotted it out, then let it appear again, making it seem to flicker like a torch. But no such explanation is really needed. Any seaman knows the tricks of the eye from prolonged watchfulness. He knows that sailors who are not sure of their exact position and are trying to make land at night are very likely to see imaginary lights and flashes, even to hear imaginary bells and breakers.

It was about two o'clock in the morning when Rodrigo de Triana, lookout on the *Pinta,* first saw something that looked like the gleam of a white, sandy cliff, standing out in the moonlight, westward, far ahead. He looked again, hard. Yes! Now there were two white cliffs and a low dark shadow that seemed to connect them. It had to be land.

"Tierra! Tierra!" screamed Rodrigo, at the top of his lungs. "Land! Land!"

With that exultant shout, Rodrigo disappears from history. No one ever heard of Rodrigo before, no one ever heard of him afterward; but his were the first European eyes—at least, the first on record—to see the New World.

This time, Captain Pinzón took time to make sure. Two weeks before he had made a bad mistake about seeing land. He was taking no chances now. This time there was no mistake. Shapes in light and shadow were gradually becoming clearer.

It was true. Land was in sight at last. They were heading straight for it.

The *Pinta's* biggest cannon had been standing, loaded and primed, ready to fire a signal the moment there was good news. Now its fat black muzzle nosed out through a porthole, just above the rolling Caribbean waves.

"Bang!" went the gun.

North America had been discovered.

Let us stop for a moment to picture, in our minds' eyes, the vast continent of North America, as it lay that moonlit night, just before the dawn broke over its Atlantic coast, then swept on westward, hour by hour, to the Pacific.

From Atlantic to Pacific, scattered tribes of Red Indians—not at all like the natives of India Columbus expected to find—lay sleeping. They could not possibly know that three little ships had anchored at San Salvador. They slept calmly—unconcerned for the future of the only way of life they could imagine. But that way of life, like everything else they knew, would now be changing.

All over North America, as the sun moved slowly west that October morning, these natives of reddish-brown skin, woke as usual. They were blissfully ignorant of the arrival of men of white skin from across the water. They did not even know of the existence of these strange people with pale faces. Only a few Indians on San Salvador now knew that.

Certainly no Indian dreamed that night, that the white man had come, to take both North and South America for his own. Nor could they guess the centuries of trouble white men would bring to them.

Columbus himself could not imagine what vast changes would now begin to sweep over geography, over history, the movements of white and Negro races, and over the whole story of mankind. The coming of three ships, which would look pathetically small to us now, bobbing in the warm blue waters, meant that the old Indian tribal life of plains, mountains, lakes and forests, was now a changing picture soon to fade.

In the southwestern part of what would one day become our own United States, the peaceful Indians of the pueblos would awake as usual. They would begin the same life they had been living for at least a thousand years. They would keep on building their large apartment houses—"pueblos"—in the rocks, worshipping their rain gods with ceremonial dances, harvesting their crops, fearing nothing—except, sometimes, raiding Apaches.

Undisturbed in their majesty, giant redwood trees, which had been growing in the time of Christ, looked through the fog toward the Pacific's waves breaking on the California coast. There were more redwoods than there are today, but some of the very trees that had been standing for centuries when Columbus landed are still standing.

From the forests of Pennsylvania to the Rockies, gigantic buffalo herds were beginning to stir in the early morning. The huge beasts grazed over plains and prairies so vast that there was enough grass and forage for all. Wolf, cougar, weasel, wildcat, lynx, and fox were nearly ready to den up for their daytime rest, after their night's hunting.

Between the Mississippi and the Pacific prowled the giant grizzlies, lords of the plains and mountains, certain of their power, unafraid of the frail red creatures on two legs who, with bows and arrows, sometimes disturbed them slightly. They could not know their fearless days were numbered now. Other two-legged creatures would be coming with weapons too deadly even for a grizzly.

Just west of the greatest river, in their leather tepees, dwelt the Sioux, a rather weak tribe, rambling on foot about the prairies. As yet, not one of their painted warriors had dreamed of horses. How could they? There were no horses in North America. Soon, white men would be bringing them. Then the Sioux would find or steal them. Possessing horses, they would become a powerful tribe, the terror of the plains, the white man's deadliest foe. Wider buffalo plains would then belong to the Sioux—for a time. But that, too, would pass.

These changes were in the future. They would not be completed for more than three hundred years. But the arrival of those three little ships, hundreds of miles away, on an ocean no Sioux had ever seen, meant that all these changes had to come.

In Mexico, only a few hundred miles to the west of the island where Columbus landed, the Aztec Indians had risen through the centuries to a fairly high point of civilization. When we say that a once savage people have risen to a degree of civilization, we mean that they have learned something about the peaceful arts; have found some kind of permanent government; have found a way of living with more grace and security than mere tribal life affords; and are at least on their way to some form of writing, though perhaps only in pictures.

Around the Great Lakes, through Canada, into New England, and down the coast of the Atlantic, ranged various tribes of the group called Algonkian—hunters, trappers, canoemen. In upper New York State, about this time, the great Iroquois leaders, Dekanáwida and Hayowentha (whose name we know as Hiawatha) were establishing the League of the Iroquois, the Five Nations. The League was just beginning to develop its power when, on that fateful morning, the ship *Pinta,* far away in southern waters, fired her signal gun, announcing the coming of a more powerful race.

Some not too distant day, the red man would lose the vast continent that had been his since the last glacier melted back into the Far North.

Such was the continent, as Columbus discovered it, in 1492. Most of these aspects of its life, Columbus himself never knew anything about. He never guessed the Sioux existed, never heard an Iroquois war whoop, never saw the towering pyramid-temples of the Aztecs. He died supposing he had found the way to India, never guessing he had found something vastly greater.

King Ferdinand and Queen Isabella gave him the title he had asked. They made him Admiral of the Ocean Sea, and decreed that the title should forever remain hereditary in his family. New Yorkers were very much astonished in the 1950's, when a Spanish warship put into the harbor on a friendly visit. One of its youngest officers—too young to command even a single ship—was Admiral of the Ocean Sea and wore an admiral's uniform. He was the living heir of the title which his ancestor, Christopher Columbus, had won.

The modern Spanish Government rightly judged that he would interest Americans.

CHAPTER 2

The Earliest Adventurers

NORTH AMERICA had been discovered long before Columbus. In one sense, the Indians had discovered it, thousands of years before, when they came from Asia—probably across Bering Strait, into Alaska, then south and east, till they occupied both North and South America. There is some reason to think that Chinese adventurers may have reached the Pacific coast, hundreds of years before Columbus; but it is all very vague, and the story may not be true. If there ever were Chinese explorers of North America, their explorations led to nothing.

Leif Ericsson, a Norse adventurer, landed in North America about the year 1000. Other Norsemen came, settled, fought the "Skraellings" —who may have been either Eskimos or Indians—then let their settlements die out. They told the rest of the world very little about North America, except that it was inhabited; that there grew in its forests such timber as they had never seen; and that the winter days were longer than in Greenland. They were so much impressed by the giant grapevines that sprawled and scrambled over the country that they call it Vineland the Good. Ericsson is supposed to have reached what is now Cambridge, Massachusetts, but no one really knows.

No Indian legend mentions the Norsemen, who left few traces. They may have built the Round Tower at Newport, Rhode Island, but it is very doubtful. They may have reached Ontario about 1000, and Minnesota in 1362. The Kensington stone, found in Minnesota in 1898, has an inscription describing a massacre of Scandinavian settlers in 1362. If the stone is genuine, a party of white men crossed half of North America 130 years before Columbus. It is certainly true that the king of Norway sent an adventurer named Paul Knudson to America, just about that time. But no one can be sure whether the Kensington stone is genuine or a fraud. Nor does anyone know what really became of Paul Knudson and his men.

It is possible that Basque and Breton fishermen had been coming to America, years before Columbus. If so, like all fishermen, having once found good fishing grounds, they preferred to keep them secret. No one can be sure about this, either.

Columbus does not need to share his glory with any of these people. None of these ancient voyagers revealed what they had found, to the civilized world as a whole. Their discoveries were more or less accidental. They made nothing of them. They came, they went, scarcely knowing what they had found. Their adventures were without result.

The Norsemen never told their stories, except in their own far northern countries. Their discoveries are recorded only in a few ancient poems, called sagas, which few Europeans could read, even then. Except for that half-hidden record, the discoveries remained unknown. Even the discoverers' fellow Norsemen forgot them. For more than three centuries, it was as if they had never made their journeys. There was, indeed, no way to spread the news. There was no printing, therefore no newspapers. The only books were manuscripts, too expensive to reach more than a few readers.

It was Christopher Columbus and the men who came after him, who opened the Western Hemisphere to the white man and his civilization.

When Columbus returned to Spain, he reported to King Ferdinand and Queen Isabella what he had found. The news astounded all Europe. The thrilling story passed swiftly from one man to another. Each sailor who had made that memorable voyage had a stirring yarn to spin. It was the most exciting story of the century, repeated innumerable times. But Columbus did not have to depend on word-of-mouth, or a few manuscripts, to spread his news. Printing had now been known to Europeans for several decades. The "news letter" in which Columbus told his story to the king and queen of Spain was the very thing the public was most eager to read.

One printer after another, all over Europe, snatched it up and ran off his own edition. Some editions were in Latin, because Latin could then be read in any country. In the New York Public Library there is a copy of the news letter, which was once valued at $8,000. Today it is worth a great deal more.

Exploration, adventure, discovery, the New World—these were the most exciting things to talk about. Tongues wagged in the market places of Europe. The Spaniards were naturally the quickest to catch the adventure-fever, since the great discoverer himself had sailed under the Spanish flag; had returned to make his report to his patrons—the Spanish king and queen. The news spread in Spain.

In 1513, only twenty-one years after Columbus, Vasco Nuñez de Balboa climbed a mountain in what he called Darien—the Isthmus of Panama. From its summit, he saw the Pacific Ocean, the real "Western Ocean Sea." He was the first white man who ever looked out across its broad expanse. Now Europeans knew that there was one more ocean to cross, before they could hope to reach China, Japan, and India, by sailing westward.

After Balboa, in 1519, Hernando Cortez landed in Mexico, conquered the great Aztec Empire, won an enormous amount of gold for himself and Spain, and established a new Spanish province. When enough Spaniards had settled to give Spanish sailors a firmly established base, it was not long before their ships were scudding boldly along the Pacific as well as the Atlantic coast of the New World. They knew now that our world was much bigger around than Columbus ever thought; but even then, did not know how big.

Columbus had led the explorers who came after him to such sights as can never be seen again. Most of them the great explorer himself never saw. But he led the way for others to wonders such as no white man had ever seen: the rich Aztec Empire in Mexico, with cities, streets, temples, sculptures, and gold; the great Inca Empire of Peru, equally civilized, equally rich; farther north, in the wild lands of North America, gigantic primitive forests that had never known the touch of steel; trees that had stood for centuries—some trees that really had stood for several thousand years; wild creatures swarming everywhere; huge grizzly bears and smaller black ones; wolves and mountain lions; vast herds of buffalo, covering the central plains almost like a huge black carpet; enormous fish in broad rivers everywhere; millions of game birds, whose flight actually darkened the sky like thunder clouds; strange, wild people, with curious arts and picturesque customs, still living in the Stone Age; a broad and beautiful land, untouched by industry, unspoiled, beautiful and natural from coast to coast, wholly undisturbed by the hand of man.

The arrival of three little ships that moonlit October night marked the beginning of a mighty change. It was a change not only on the American continents but in the whole world picture and the course of all history. It was a change that has never stopped.

In a short time, men who had never traveled anywhere, all sorts of men who knew nothing of sailing or geography or the hard, rough life of an explorer in a new and primitive land, wanted to be explorers, too. Mingled with them, were experienced sailors and tough Spanish soldiers.

Many of these people were stirred, not by any real desire for adventure or discovery, but by mere eagerness to "get rich quick." The New World, they felt sure, must be full of gold, as Mexico and Peru had been. Ideas of the vast wealth of the new lands buzzed in their heads like gnats. (Even now, after five hundred years, the idea still abides. Most Europeans still believe that everyone in North America is rich.)

A glance at the map will show how natural it was that the first exploration beyond the island where Columbus landed should begin in and around the Gulf of Mexico. We still call the islands there the West Indies. It was natural, too, that from these islands, Spanish explorers should go on to the Gulf Coast, the whole northern part of which is now United States territory. It was just as natural for the men who made these daring explorations to expect to find more rich cities, like those in Mexico and Peru. If they existed south and west, why not to the north as well? Eagerly the Spaniards plunged into the forests and across the plains that were one day to become the United States of America.

But North America was not in the least like Mexico or Peru. The Spaniards, who were the first white men to explore the interior, met with disappointment and disillusion, so far as wealth and riches were concerned. The natural wonders they beheld, the strange ways of the red man's life were such marvels as will never be seen again. The Spaniards did not care. These men wanted only gold. The first Spanish explorers were so mad for it, they could not realize the possibilities of much greater wealth that lay before them—wealth vaster than any gold mine could produce: the wealth of the forests, riches in iron, coal, and copper, the fertile soil of the plains, the abundance of future American farms, the tremendous future industry that was to astound the world—to all these things they were wholly blind. They did not even understand that such miracles would all be possible—some day.

A picture of the North American continent as the first white adventurers saw it is really several pictures of the different sections of the continent. We can see these pictures only from descriptions that were written down by some of those explorers in their notes and journals. Sometimes the notes they left are scanty, sometimes full. Only by piecing them together can we learn what each part of our country was like, when the first white men saw it.

Descriptions are few, because the explorers did not come for the special purpose of reporting what they saw. They came to find gold and riches. They were not reporters; neither were they men trained in observation; and they were not writers.

Also, these first explorers traveled through great hardships and often at great risk. Much of the time, they were almost exhausted by the effort just to stay alive. They had to find their own food. They had to build their own shelters. They had to try to make friends with the natives—Indians whose language they could not understand. If they could not make friends, they had to fight. Always they were under the strain of constant danger, constant watchfulness. They had little energy left to sit down and write about what they saw. A few of them did. Many others wrote what they remembered, after they got home. One or two expeditions even took artists along, whose pictures are wonderful memorials of scenes that no one now will ever see again.

CHAPTER 3

The Red Man's Dixie

BECAUSE the Spaniards were the first to push inland into North America from the seashore, the earliest descriptions of the modern United States as it then was, are all by Spaniards. It is surprising, reading them, to see in how many ways the "Red Man's Dixie" was like the Dixie we sing about today. All the rest of North America has changed enormously. So, of course, have the southern states. But what was one day to be called Dixieland already possessed, even before Columbus, many of the delightful characteristics for which it is still known.

Even in these primitive times, early white travelers found southern cooking the best in North America. The southern Indians had as many different kinds of food as the English. We know this through the traveler and trader, James Adair, who lived among them when they were still wild. He says their food was of a kind a white man could thoroughly enjoy. (The meals of western and northern Indians sometimes nauseated their white guests.)

These Indians of Dixie were too particular to use ordinary corn, to grind into meal. They insisted on making their cornmeal flour only from kernels of white corn. Yellow corn was not good enough. They also used a special flour of mixed corn, beans, and potatoes, ground together. Refined by sifting through sieves of cane, this made very good bread—baked either in thin cakes moistened with bear's oil, or in large loaves, placed on the hot earth where a campfire had been, and then covered with an earthen pot and hot coals. Adair, who often watched the southern squaws at work, says that their baking was as clean as that in any white woman's oven. When the loaves were done, the squaws washed them with warm water and they became firm and white.

In their warm and productive part of North America, the southern Indians had all sorts of vegetable foods and fruits. Their squaws boiled or roasted sweet potatoes and other root vegetables. Pumpkins were barbecued over a fire. Persimmons were dried, mashed with parched corn, and baked into cakes, which were then cooked with venison fat, or bear's oil. The Indians also sun-dried black mulberries to store away. Berries thus preserved could be cooked as needed, with bread, parched cornmeal, and oil. Oranges became abundant later, and the Indians grew them in groves which sometimes covered several acres. The fruit was roasted and, since it was much sourer than the improved varieties we eat today, the Indians sometimes opened it and filled it with honey.

It was, in other ways however, a very different Dixieland from the one we know. The whole South was one great forest from the Atlantic coast to the Mississippi River and the Gulf of Mexico. In the Shenandoah Valley of Virginia, as in parts of the Middle West, the Indians had for years kept places, where the ground was level, burned free of trees so they could see the game animals more easily. Meadowland and river valleys were covered with canebrakes and waving grass, through which wandered buffalo, elk, and deer pursued by wolves and panthers, while foxes preyed upon smaller animals.

Beginning with the Ohio, Shenandoah, and Kentucky rivers, and on southward, the valleys everywhere were covered with a luxuriant growth of cane. No one, for the last hundred years, has seen anything like these tremendous brakes, whose tasseled tops once waved over mile upon mile of fertile plains. Most of them soon disappeared because the first white settlers were quick to realize that a flourishing canebrake was a sign of first-class farmland. The soil was good, with the added advantage that the stalks, which could be slashed away like corn, were much easier to clear than thick-set forest trees.

A single canebrake in that luxuriant Southland might extend along a river for a hundred miles with a width of two or three miles, filling whole valleys and crowding out all other plant life. The jointed stalks were enormously strong and tall, sometimes reaching thirty, occasionally, forty feet. The leaves were long and green, like corn. The tops were tasseled. The stalks of cane themselves were so strong and so rigid that, with their ends sharpened, the Indians could use them to spear fish. Broken, they were razor-sharp. A "cane-stab"—a wound made by stepping on a stub left erect in the ground—was one of the most dreaded of injuries. So sharp was the outer glasslike cortex that the Indians, lacking flint, sometimes improvised knives from its sharp edges. Faggots of dried cane made convenient torches, which gave illumination to their wild midnight dances.

Canebrakes were perfect hiding places, too. A large one could easily hide a man on horseback. Many records tell of white pioneers who escaped the Indians only by diving in time into a handy tangle of cane. They tell of Indians who escaped white men in the same way. Once a man was thus hidden, there was no way to find him. A canebrake on one occasion saved Daniel Boone from redskins who had killed his brother.

But even cane could not crowd out the trees. Both banks of the Mississippi River were forests all the way to the sea, except where the Indians had cleared away occasional fields for corn and beans. Cottonwood, poplar, cane, tangles of brier and grapevine edged both banks of the river in the southern part of the valley. Five or six miles back from the river, where water was not quite so plentiful as in the sodden bottom lands, open prairie began, with mulberry and persimmon trees —and with vines still climbing everywhere.

Farther west, along prairie streams, cottonwoods and willows were very nearly the only trees. But along the southern Mississippi and its tributaries trees of many kinds reached such dimensions that the

Indians—and later, white men, too—could find trunks big enough to make dugout canoes forty and fifty feet long, with a beam of three feet or more. Here also grapes hung from the vines that clung to the trees, and a hungry or thirsty traveler, without even leaving his canoe, could pick them as they overhung the river.

The menace of winter famine, which always troubled the northern tribes, was unknown. Sassafras and wild cinnamon flavored the bear fat that Indians kept, from winter to winter, in earthen jars. Sometimes they stored food in calabashes. Fields of corn spread in all directions. In this warm climate, the land produced two crops a year. Southern Indians raised about the same ones as their northern brothers —corn, potatoes, tobacco, beans, peas, melons, squashes, sunflowers, pumpkins, called "pompions" by some of the early white travelers.

Deer were as common here as they were everywhere. Pigeons were even more plentiful than wild ducks and wild geese. Waterfowl, after nesting in the northern United States and Canada, came south in winter, in the vast numbers then common in North America. They flew in flocks so large that one white traveler said they looked like clouds approaching through the air. When huge flocks were disturbed, they took wing like a great dark thunderstorm. The beating of their wings, their quacking and squalling, together with the confusion of so many fluttering bodies, made a deafening noise. They were so fearless that one white hunter was astonished to find that they were preparing to attack *him,* because he was nearing their nests.

Into this wild and luxuriant land by way of its most luxuriant part— the Florida peninsula—the first Spanish explorers came. They were not much interested in the fertile acres they passed over, because their heads were filled with fantastic dreams of rich empires they were going to loot.

The first of these visitors, however, was not seeking wealth but health. In 1513, only twenty-one years after Columbus, Juan Ponce de León visited Florida, hunting for a miraculous fountain of eternal youth, described in Indian legends. Whoever drank the water of this marvelous spring, the legends said, would never grow old. Needless to say, Ponce de León never found the wonderful fountain, nor did he leave any written record of all the interesting things he must have seen in primitive Florida.

Four years later, Francisco Fernández de Córdoba, after he had landed in Yucatán and had been driven off by fierce Indian warriors, allowed his pilot, who had been with Ponce de León, to take him to Florida, too. But he, also, left almost no description of what he saw.

As early as 1521, there were many Spanish slave raiders sailing along our Atlantic coast in search of Indians to capture and take home as slaves. They left no records, either.

As early as 1526, the Spaniards made an attempt to start a colony in southeastern United States. This first attempt was led by Vásquez de Ayllón. After hunting for gold and jewels near Cape Fear, he and his men spent a bad winter along a river in South Carolina. About 150 of his men got home to Spain alive, but they left their leader, Ayllón, dead in the wilderness.

Within the next few years—fifty years after Columbus—white adventurers were drawn to the strange new country as moths to a bright light. Two or more expeditions were exploring in different parts of the country at the same time. With some of those early explorers came missionaries and people who intended to stay and start colonies in the New World.

While De Soto was exploring our South, 1539-1542, Coronado was looking for gold in our Southwest, 1540-1542, penetrating as far as modern Kansas. While Coronado explored ashore, Alarcón was sailing up the Gulf of Mexico, 1540, thinking, mistakenly, that he was traveling parallel to Coronado's inland march. Other Spaniards began to sniff along the California coast.

On the Atlantic coast, Cartier was sailing into the great Gulf of the St. Lawrence and up the river, in the southeastern corner of Canada. He began a series of French explorations that, in time, would reach halfway across the continent and down to the Gulf of Mexico.

The first of these early explorers, whose exploits can be more fully described, arrived in Florida in 1528, thirty-six years after Columbus's first voyage led the way. This was Captain Pánfilo de Narváez.

CHAPTER 4

Narváez and Cabeza de Vaca
1528–1536

CAPTAIN Pánfilo de Narváez was an adventurer who looked the part—looked, indeed, like a pirate. He had a red beard and only one eye, having lost the other fighting against Cortez. His formidable appearance was enhanced by a deep bass voice.

Narváez landed on the west side of Tampa Bay, in Florida, in April, 1528. With him came four hundred men, hoping to make their fortunes in the New World; but all save five were doomed to die with their commander in this unknown country.

Sailing up the Gulf Coast, Narváez and his soldiers were the first white men to see primitive, unspoiled Florida. At least, they were the first white men a few of whom got home alive to tell about it. There had certainly been one ship before them. No one knows whose ship it was. Everyone on board seems to have perished. Narváez found only a few traces of it, a little later.

Before the Spaniards, as they looked out from their ships, lay a vast expanse of absolutely wild country, covered with forests, large lakes, swamps, and stagnant water. They could see there was abundant timber of many kinds, particularly pine, cedar, palms, cypress, and chestnut. Above all there was sassafras. This fragrant tree is purely American. It does not grow in Europe, at all. Later European explorers got the idea that it was a wonderful cure for all sorts of diseases, probably because it smells so good and can be used to make a kind of tea. There were also many plants such as wild cotton, hemp, and flax.

To travelers accustomed to Europe's crowded cities, clustering villages, and cultivated fields, this thick, wild jungle growth of trees and vines was an amazing sight. But however beautiful and wonderful it may have been, it was not what interested Narváez and his conquistadors—that is, "conquerors," as they liked to call themselves. These rough adventurers were not interested in luxuriant, wild beauties of Nature. Gold and jewels were what they were after. They were looking for rich cities to loot.

Where, in this wild riot of Nature, were the people? Where were the cities? Where was the wealth? Where were the jewels? Where was the gold? All they saw were a few scattered Indian villages.

The first village at which they landed was completely empty. The frightened inhabitants had fled when they saw strangers approaching. The site of this village can still be located by enormous mounds of shells, left from ancient Indian feasts. One of the soldiers, rummaging through the Indians' abandoned fishing nets, found a gold object, described as a rattle, or "tinklet." This, and a few other gold articles, easily convinced Narváez that he was about to come to an empire of great wealth, even if, thus far, he had found only forests and occasional villages. This was what he wanted to believe—so he believed it.

He sent scouts on ahead, who pushed north into Old Tampa Bay, and there caught a few Timucuas—a tribe that died out two hundred years ago. These natives led the Spaniards to another Indian village, where they found many boxes such as Spaniards used for wool, linen, canvas, cloth, iron, and other merchandise. These boxes had plainly come from Europe, and the Indians explained by signs that they had been taken from a ship, wrecked in Tampa Bay. No one has ever found out whose ship this was.

When the Spaniards inquired by signs where the gold objects came from, the Timucuas said "Apalachen" and pointed north. The Apalachee tribe lived in northwestern Florida, around what were to become the future cities of Pensacola, Tallahassee, and St. Marks. This tribe, too, died out a long time ago, but their name is preserved by the Appalachian Mountains and a few other geographic names. The Apalachee got some of their gold by barter with the Indians of northern Georgia, where nuggets were washed out of the river sands. There was also a little gold in Florida, though Narváez never found it. To those Indians a bit of bright gold was nothing but a pretty ornament, which they cherished for that reason only. They had no idea of its value to white men.

The town of Apalachee was probably on Lake Miccosukee, just south of the Florida-Georgia border. Narváez rashly struck out through the strange country to find it, leaving only vague orders for his ships to go to a certain harbor which he had been told lay farther up the coast. They were to wait there for him. If he did not appear, the ships were to remain nearby while some of the crews searched the country for him for a year before giving up.

As the harbor Narváez had in mind lay to the south instead of to the north, it is no wonder that he and his expedition never saw their ships again.

It was early May when Narváez started north, keeping close to the seacoast to avoid the worst of the Florida swamps. At first he did not find the going very hard, as the country was level and sandy, broken here and there by clumps of tall pines. But when swamps, creeks, and rivers lay across their path, the Spaniards found it slow, difficult work. Fallen trees and tangled reeds made a network, obstructing the waterways. This was alligator country, too, and it was spring, the mating season. The terrifying roars of big bull alligators must have sounded on every side.

When the column of adventurers reached the vicinity of the Witlacoochee River, a junior officer of noble blood, named Cabeza de Vaca, was sent to the coast to look for the ships. He and the men with him had to wade part of the time, treading on oysters which cut their feet badly. They returned to report failure. They found the river's mouth, but no sign of the ships. Cabeza de Vaca was destined to become the most famous member of the Narváez expedition. He was one of the few who returned to Spain alive, and it was he who wrote down their terrible story.

Up to mid-June the Spaniards had seen only a few Indians. Then they were startled one day by the sound of music coming from the woods ahead. Presently Indians appeared, escorting their local chief and, as was the custom among many of the southern Indians, advancing to greet their visitors with music played on flutes made of hollow reeds.

The chief offered to go with them to Apalachee. It took a whole day to make a rough canoe and ferry the men across the wide and swift Suwanee River. One man and one horse drowned. The Spaniards, who seem to have done very little hunting, were by this time so hungry for fresh meat that they ate the horse for supper that night.

North of the river, the country became very difficult for men on foot, though it was wonderfully beautiful to see. The forest was thick with towering trees. So many had fallen that it was a weary task for the Spaniards to climb over them or walk long distances around their trunks. Not only had many of the trees fallen, but it was easy to see the marks of the lightning that had riven other trees, still standing, from top to bottom.

As they struggled through this densely tangled forest, the Spaniards luckily escaped the dangerous reptiles of that primitive country. Of these, the worst three were the big diamondback rattlesnakes, the small but deadly coral snakes, and water moccasins, though these last were no great danger to troops, except when they crossed water. In Florida, the diamondbacks live in pine swamps and hummock lands, through both of which the adventurers passed. The coral snake lives under the decayed leaves and wood of the forest floor. There is no record that anyone died from snakebite, probably because the Spaniards made so much noise they frightened the reptiles into hiding.

The Spaniards took possession easily of the little town of Apalachee, for Narváez had the luck to arrive when all the men were absent. When the warriors came home, they were taken by surprise and easily driven off. The village contained corn, both fresh and dried, which the Indians were saving for their own use. This the hungry invaders seized immediately.

After all that he had heard about it, Apalachee was no more a city than any of the other Indian villages Narváez had seen. It was only a cluster of about forty thatched huts, surrounded by dense woods and fresh-water lakes.

Not all the land was forest. There were many cornfields and fine open pastures to attract deer, of which there were three species. Geese, ducks, herons swarmed on the lakes, and the woods were full of partridges, rabbits, hares, bears, cougars. Here the Spaniards saw their first opossum. They thought this animal with a pouch in which to carry its babies most remarkable, and Europeans for the next two hundred years continued to marvel at it.

After only a month of this kind of travel, Narváez had had enough. For one thing, his army was not dressed for it. Spanish armor might save a man's life in battle but it was a clumsy and uncomfortable uniform to wear clanking through hot thick forests and wading through swamps. Even if the men took off their armor, they still had to lug the sharp, heavy, awkward steel plates with them as they marched.

Friendly Indians told Narváez that beyond Apalachee there were very few people, while to the west lay great lakes, more dense forests, and immense deserts. In all this wilderness, there was still no trace of the rich cities he had hoped to find. Narváez decided to go southward, to the coastal town of Aute, near the present town of St. Marks.

The first day, the Indians allowed them to go unmolested. Then, waiting until the Spaniards were struggling through a lake tangled with snags and fallen trees, floundering in water up to their chests, the Indians sent a shower of arrows at the invaders, while they themselves hid behind trees on the shore. These Tumucua Indians were big, powerful men. One of their skeletons, dug up in modern times, was seven feet tall. Their bows were thick as a man's arm. Pointed with snake teeth, bone, or flint, their long reed arrows went straight through steel. Against such weapons, the Spaniards found their European armor was no protection. Some dead Spaniards were found with their bodies pierced from side to side with arrows. One man died from an arrow straight through the neck.

In open country the Spaniards on horses could have chased and scattered the Indians, but the natives were clever enough to make their attacks in dense woods, where a mounted man could not move.

In spite of everything, Narváez got most of his men through to the coast. At St. Marks Bay, he halted. There was no sign of his ships. He must have known by that time there never would be. The expedition was plainly a failure. His big problem now was how to get away. Giving up hope of his ships, he decided to build boats in which to sail along the shore of the Gulf to the Spanish colonies in Mexico.

It is hard to believe that the despairing Spaniards could make boats at all, for they had few tools and no supplies. But these were desperate men, caught a long, long way from home, in a primitive country, with nothing but great forests, water, and hostile Indians around them. They had to build those boats or die. By terrible exertions, they did manage to produce a crude little fleet.

To get iron, they collected such things as stirrups, spurs, crossbows, melted them down, and made them into nails, rude saws, and axes. The tools were bad and clumsy, but the Spaniards, in their terrible predicament, made them serve. The blacksmith used an awkward bellows, made of wood pipes and deerskins. Somehow, these desperate men made bellows pipes out of logs, though they had no augurs long enough to bore them. They must have split the logs in quarters, chopped out the centers, then bound the four sections back together with leather thongs.

In time, they cut enough timber for five boats and calked the seams with palmetto fiber. They robbed the Indians of several hundred bushels of corn and gathered shellfish at the risk of their lives, with Indians sniping at them whenever they could. They ate their horses after having carefully worked cylinders of hide off the legs. They used these for water bottles.

At last, when all this painful labor was over, the expedition pushed out from St. Marks to sea. Their crazy, unseaworthy craft were crowded with men. The gunwales were nearly awash, at best only a few inches above the water. Propelled by oars and by sails made from shirts, the boats managed to creep along the coast for a month, occasionally seeing a few Indian fishermen.

There came a time when their drinking water was used up. According to Cabeza de Vaca's story, they had gone five days without water when they met a fleet of canoes filled with friendly Indians. The chief, wearing a robe made of civet marten still fragrant with the animal's musk, greeted them. The white men, parched with thirst, decided to take a chance and visit the Indian village. There they saw clay pitchers containing water before each dwelling. Besides fresh water, the Indians gave them cooked fish. In return, Narváez gave the natives dried corn and trinkets.

About midnight, in spite of all their early friendliness, the Indians suddenly attacked the Spaniards. Before dawn, the white men had to stand off two more attacks. They were prevented from putting back to sea by the weather, which had turned rough. There was nothing to do but huddle by the shore and wait.

When the weather improved, Narváez and his desperate Spaniards packed themselves into their boats once more, and crawled along the coast again. They passed what they called a "broad" river, which may have been the Mississippi. The leader, having the best boat crew, finally called across the waves that each should do what he thought best to save his own life. That, he called out, was what he was now going to do himself. With these words, Narváez turned away from his men and abandoned his command. He was soon blown out into the Gulf of Mexico and never seen again. The other boats gradually drifted apart and most of them disappeared. Though there were still a few surviving Spaniards, the expedition itself had come to an inglorious end.

As a leader, Narváez had been incompetent. He had neither planned his expedition carefully, nor had he provided enough supplies. He was totally unprepared for the hardships of the country he was about to explore. His arrangements for having his ships meet him had been foolishly indefinite, both as to time, and even place of meeting. Moreover, he was a bad commander. Considering the kind of incompetent brute he was, that is not surprising. Far too many of the Spanish conquistadors were brutal in the extreme. But Narváez was remarkable for brutality even among brutes. On one occasion he sat on his horse and calmly watched his men butcher two thousand friendly and defenseless Indians, just because it amused them! The Indians had done nothing to them. The Spaniards just felt like killing.

Cabeza de Vaca, who lived to write the terrible story, struggled on in his own small craft, in company with one other boat, until they were blown away from each other in a storm. According to his reckoning, it was November 6, 1528, when a great wave tossed his lonely little boat up on the beach, somewhere near Galveston, Texas, perhaps on San Luis Island, southwest of Galveston Island. Friendly Indians appeared, bringing food, but that was the end of the white men's good luck. When, after several days' rest, they tried to launch their boat again, it turned bottom up, killing three. The few who escaped drowning were now stranded.

With dread in their hearts, they followed the Indians to their village. It was an invitation they were afraid to decline. Some of the Spaniards feared they would be sacrificed to the gods, in the cruel Aztec way—which was to slash open the breast and tear the heart from the living victim—but they had to go. There was nothing else they could do.

Fortunately, the Indians continued hospitable and friendly. Presently, de Vaca noticed that one of them was wearing a European ornament, which he knew his own party had not given. Where could the man have gotten it? When he inquired by signs, an Indian pointed back the way they had come. The ornament had come from other white men, over there. Cabeza de Vaca sent two Spaniards and two Indians in that direction, to find out who these survivors were. His messengers had hardly left the village, when they met Spaniards from a second boat, who had also escaped alive. Having heard of Cabeza de Vaca's party, they had come to look for them.

Of the few men now remaining from the Narváez expedition, the four healthiest were selected to work their way on foot west to Mexico, while the others settled down to live with the Indians until help reached them. But the valiant four were never heard of again. The Spaniards left behind waited in vain for a sign of rescue which never came. Most of them died, one by one, in that cruel country.

To make matters worse, bad weather set in. Food ran short for red and white men alike. Some of the Spaniards horrified the Indians by resorting to cannibalism. Then came the time when only fifteen of the original eighty white survivors were left.

For some unexplained reason, Indian kindness gradually ceased. The redskins made slaves of the Spaniards, whom they now treated horribly. Finally, Cabeza de Vaca escaped alone to another and more friendly band of Indians, somewhere in Texas, and set himself up as a trader. What he used to trade with, he does not say. In time, he located three scattered survivors of the expedition, including Estebánico, a Negro slave of the Spaniards, who had been born in Morocco. These four wandered with Indians in search of prickly pears for food. They suffered agonies from mosquitoes. Cabeza de Vaca wrote, much later, that there is no torment in the world to equal that produced by swarms of these shrill-voiced insects.

These four were the first Europeans to see the American buffalo, running wild. (Cortez had seen one or two in the zoo of the Aztec ruler, Montezuma.) Cabeza called them hunch-backed cows. He thought their meat was finer and fatter than the beef in Spain. He does not seem ever to have known of the immense buffalo herds of the Great Plains, farther north.

The irony of the whole expedition was that, moving across the Gulf in their small boats, Narváez and his hapless adventurers had sailed past the fertile, fruitful country of the broad coastal plains, east of the Mississippi, where they could have found food. Instead of landing there, when they had the chance, they had gone on from one disaster to another until the handful of Spaniards that were left found themselves ashore west of the Mississippi on the desolate Texas plains, where even Indians found it hard to survive. Had they been farther north, they might have eaten abundantly of buffalo steaks, but they did not know that, and few buffalo ever roamed so far south as the Texas coast, to which the travelers clung as their only guide. Somewhere along that coast, they knew, were the Spanish colonies for which they sought. But the colonies were far to the west and south. The Gulf Coast was a long way round.

Sometime in September of 1533, five years after the Narváez expedition had landed in the New World—five years of extreme dangers,

hardships, and disappointments—the three surviving Spaniards re-
solved to make another attempt to break away from their savage existence. They took the Negro, Estebánico, and fled west across the
plains. They fell in with friendly Indians. When some of the Indians
complained of headaches, one of the Spaniards made the sign of the
Cross over them and commended them to God. The redskins were instantly cured and, in gratitude, brought presents of prickly pears and
deer meat.

Meantime, in the northern part of Mexico, whither the four anxious
fugitives were making their way, a certain Nuño de Guzmán, an enemy of Cortez, had made himself supreme. Nuño de Guzmán was a
violent and bloody man, greedy for loot and slaves. In April of 1536,
a troop of his cavalry was moving along the Sinaloa River, in what is
now the Mexican province of Sinaloa.

One day, a mounted patrol of four men, scouting along the river,
beheld in amazement a white man and Negro, both with heavy beards,
coming toward them out of the north. There was an escort of Indians
with these two astonishing men.

The troopers stood staring at Cabeza de Vaca and Estebánico for a
long time. They could not believe their eyes. More astonishing still,
one of the strange ragged creatures asked them in good Spanish to take
him to their commanding officer. The soldiers took both of the fugitives back to their camp. Then the commander sent three of his
troopers and some Indians, with Estebánico as guide, to bring the
other two Spaniards who were following some twenty-five miles behind. Safe now at last, under military escort, they went on to Mexico
City to be received by an astonished viceroy. After eight years of
struggle, this was the end of the Narváez expedition.

CHAPTER 5

De Soto in the South

AFTER Columbus had proved that a voyage westward to new lands was possible, other Spanish explorers quickly followed. They were dazzled by what they found, for the Aztec and Inca civilizations of Mexico and South America had built great cities, achieved immense wealth, and developed a remarkable culture. The huge stores of gold that Cortez had seized in Mexico and Pizarro in Peru fired the imagination and the greed of other Spaniards. If South America and Mexico possessed such wealth, why not the American lands lying beyond them to the north?

One of these men, eager for adventure, fame, and wealth, was Ferdinand De Soto. He had been with Pizarro in Peru, had fought in Nicaragua, and had come home to Spain so rich that even royalty condescended to borrow money from him. Now he hoped to grow still richer in North America. He thought it only reasonable to expect another native empire, abounding in gold and jewels, to the north.

The queer thing is that De Soto still retained these ardent hopes, even after the bedraggled Cabeza de Vaca had returned to Spain with his tale of suffering and privation. But De Soto suspected de Vaca of not telling the whole truth. He thought he was keeping something to himself, or that he had been "sworn not to divulge certain things."

Ferdinand De Soto was an experienced conquistador, and, like Narváez and most of the others, he was a good deal of a brute as well. He enjoyed "the sport of hunting Indians." He had an ugly habit of throwing natives who displeased him to his pack of savage dogs, to be torn to pieces. He burned one Indian alive, while the poor wretch's tribe looked on in horror, because the brave and loyal redskin refused to betray the hiding place of his chief. When the others, too, stood firm, he burned them all. De Soto also went in for slashing off hands and noses of red men as minor punishments, and he had no hesitation about sentencing even his white followers to hanging or beheading, when he wanted to give a lesson in discipline.

However, De Soto was no worse than other Spaniards of those days, who thought nothing of beheading Indians just to test the sharpness of their Spanish blades and their own mastery of the sword! De Soto was indeed something more than a mere greedy brute. He was also a bold and skillful leader.

When De Soto set out for the New World, he went far better equipped than Narváez. With six hundred soldiers, 213 horses, a pack of fighting hounds, and—wonderful to relate—a herd of swine, De Soto landed in Florida, May 28, 1539, either at Tampa Bay or at Charlotte Harbor, farther south. No one has ever understood why he chose the very country where the Narváez expedition had found nothing but disaster.

De Soto took his pigs along, so as to be sure of food. As a result, he and his men were never hungry, as the Narváez expedition had been. Starting with thirteen pigs, he bred them on the march, so that by the following spring he had three hundred. Six months later, they had increased to five hundred. By the time De Soto died, on the bank of the Mississippi, three years after his arrival in Florida, his own share of the pigs numbered seven hundred!

What an amazing parade De Soto's march must have been! Imagine a sight so strange and fantastic as Spanish cavalrymen in full armor, lances in hand, riding their horses and leading sturdy Spanish infantry, who in turn were followed by a baggage train and then by chained Indian slaves, who carefully herded the squealing pigs through the thick forests and alligator-infested swamps of Florida. They carried the pigs in canoes across the Mississippi and scrambled with them over the plains. Glance at the map and see where they marched— north, then south and west, and east again, with their pork dinners trotting along behind!

There had never been such a march in any exploration anywhere in the world. It must have been astonishing to see, and even more astonishing to hear. The Indians must have gazed in wonder at the long lines of metal men riding upon strange animals, and followed by smaller animals still more strange.

With quartermaster supplies like that, grunting along behind the marching column, De Soto's expedition could not starve. Learning from the white men, the Indians took to raising pigs themselves. Some pigs escaped and ran wild. It is said that the vicious and dangerous wild hogs that still lurk in the Okefenokee Swamp—known there as "piney woods rooters"—are descended from De Soto's droves in Georgia. Through centuries, they have grown huge and savage on the lush vegetation. Perhaps the pigs, which are deadly snake-killers, help to explain why the expedition did not suffer from snake bites. De Soto seems to have lost no men at all from venomous reptiles with which the country swarmed.

Shortly after they landed, some of De Soto's men who were pursuing Indians, were astonished to hear one of them shout in Spanish to the nearest horseman, "Do not slay me, cavalier; I am a Christian!" They had had the good fortune to find the last survivor of the Narváez expedition, Juan Ortiz, nobleman of Seville.

It was a great piece of luck. Previously, the Spaniards had had no way of talking to the Indians. Ortiz, having lived so long among them, had almost forgotten how to speak his own language but he soon recovered it and became an almost perfect interpreter. He was no use as a guide, however, because like the Indians themselves, he knew nothing of the country fifty or sixty miles from his own village.

When De Soto found that neither Ortiz nor the Indians could tell him anything about cities filled with gold, he sent out a reconnoitering party; but all it found was more wild, thickly wooded country, low, very wet, with many ponds. For a while, food was short because De Soto was saving his pigs to breed. The troops ate watercress, corn, cabbage palm. When they discovered the wild American chestnuts, they thought they were delicious.

More or less following the trail of Narváez, they pushed on to Apalachee. Sometimes the Indians greeted them with the flute-playing that had greeted Narváez, but more often they fought. Captured Indians were put in chains and used as slaves to carry baggage.

As they marched north, the Spaniards continued to find the natives raising corn, pumpkins, beans, cucumbers, and plums. (Old plum orchards still mark a forgotten Indian village.) Once De Soto hid his written notes in a pumpkin along the trail, leaving a sign above it, so that the soldiers following him could find it.

In October, they found the place, near St. Marks, where Narváez had built his boats. Remnants of troughs were still there, and also skulls of the horses that had eaten from them. Here De Soto spent the winter and during this time the pigs had their little ones.

In March, 1540, the expedition started on north again. In Georgia, the Spaniards found the country picturesque, with plenty of water and luxuriant growth. All along the way, from the moment they landed in Florida, and far on into Georgia and the Carolinas, they were admiring the longleaf pine trees, which they thought were as tall as the pines of Spain. Northern Georgia and South Carolina country they found delightful and fertile; they were pleased with the open forests with nut trees and mulberries, which were even better than those of Spain. Sometimes the long column passed large, empty spaces, overgrown with grass, where villages had once stood. Indians told them they had been abandoned because of a pestilence two years before.

The Indians here never lacked meat. They had plenty of deer, wild turkeys, rabbits, and other game. But De Soto's six hundred men, since they were not hunters, and since their commander was still saving his pigs for emergencies, were often glad to eat dogs.

Sometimes, powerful local chiefs helped the expedition. One chief sent a single carrying party of four hundred Indians. Only Indian baggage carriers knew how to get through the narrow, winding forest trails. There was no beast of burden in all North America, except the dog, which plains tribes sometimes used as a pack animal and sometimes to draw a travois. The travois was a simple arrangement of two long sticks tied to the animal's shoulders, with the other ends dragging on the ground. Across these the Indians fastened sticks or hides, on which they placed their bundles. Wheels had not been invented in the Western Hemisphere. Dogs, though better than nothing on the plains, were not much use in the eastern forests.

Another chief sent two thousand Indians, loaded with rabbits, partridges, cornbread, two wild turkeys and many dogs. A Cherokee chief in North Carolina sent a gift of seven hundred turkeys. These gifts were probably made in the hope that the invading white men would not molest the donors or steal from them.

The wild turkeys that flourished in primitive America were very good eating. Later, the American pioneers ate slices of the white breast meat instead of the bread they could not get in the wilderness. Wild turkeys then were about as large as the biggest domesticated ones of today. A really big gobbler might stand three feet high and weigh twenty to forty pounds. There have been stories of fifty-pound birds being caught in the north. In March and April, they made the early mornings ring with their shrill gobbling from the magnolia trees in which they roosted.

In Georgia, De Soto entered the territory of the Creek Confederacy, a group of Indian tribes which had achieved something almost like civilization. They lived a life of security and comfort, though they did not have the boundless wealth De Soto was after. They were governed by powerful chiefs, some of whom were women. They had learned how to grow their own food, and dressed in white garments described as linen. These tribes made good cloth out of mulberry bark, and they also used the fibres of wild hemp and wild flax.

They lived in neat cabins with gabled roofs, built partly of planks and partly of bark and saplings. Since the Indians had no iron to make saws, they split their planks from tree trunks with wooden wedges—something the northern tribes never learned to do. The houses were plastered, inside and out, with a tough mortar held together with grass. To confuse raiding enemies, these Indians used an extraordinary device. First they made loopholes in the walls of each house, through which they could fire their arrows, then they plastered the holes over on the outside. An approaching foe, unable to see the loopholes, would have no idea the houses were defensible. Inside, each loophole was carefully indicated by a circle. At the critical moment, the warriors punched through the holes and shot their arrows.

Being made largely of cypress planking, fastened to southern pine, locust, or sassafras logs driven into the ground, these houses were almost indestructible. All the enemy could do was to try to set them on fire. But that was difficult. Ordinary cabins burned easily. But the plaster-covered wood resisted fire.

Their cabins were whitewashed with crushed oyster shells—later to be used by white settlers as a substitute for lime—or else with white chalk or white clay. A prosperous warrior's household would have a corncrib—the design of which the whites later imitated.

The dwellings were furnished inside with couches raised from the ground on forked sticks, to make it harder for swarming fleas to reach the sleepers. The couches were covered with cane, then with mattresses filled with cane splinters, and finally with buffalo, panther, bear, elk, or deerskins, dressed with the hair on, to make them soft as velvet.

To ensure their growing up with suitable virtues, boy babies were put to bed on panther skins, little girls on the skins of fawns or buffalo calves.

Floors were covered with carpets woven from wild hemp, painted in bright designs. Yarn spun from buffalo wool was used as a base for beadwork. The Choctaws made blankets of turkey feathers twisted into hemp thread.

Some of the clothing of these southern Indians would seem luxurious to modern white men. They knew how to tan skins beautifully, so that they were soft and delicate to touch. The summer visiting costume of the warriors was a shirt of deerskin, dressed in this way. Winter hunting clothes were made of otter or beaver—skins that would cost thousands of dollars today but that were ordinary clothes to the savages. They cared so little about the fur that they wore it inside, as in a fur-lined coat, caring nothing about the glossy beauty of the pelts.

All men wore the breechclout, for the Indians had no use at all for the pinching of trousers. Hunters wore high deerskin leggings reaching up to long hunting coats, which protected them among brambles, twigs, and underbrush. Southern tribes went barefoot when possible; but in cold weather they protected their feet with moccasins of bear or elk skin.

Headdresses were as important to them as they were to the western Indians, but they were different in design. They were not the long, flowing bonnets of eagle feathers worn by the Sioux, Blackfeet, and others. Instead, these headdresses were made of swan's feathers. The first white men called them "crowns."

The southern tribes had an advanced agriculture, cultivating many fine fields, in which they raised the usual Indian crops, including two kinds of corn—yellow for eating, white for flour. Near each Indian dwelling was a small field, fenced with saplings fastened to stakes in the ground. More distant fields, too big to fence, were not planted until the wild fruit began to ripen, drawing the birds away from the new seed.

Everybody shared in the planting of the large community fields. They made a ceremony and party of it. The planting date was always set by an old warrior whose ceremonial title was "old beloved man." He notified his village the day before the planting was to begin. Everyone, including the highest chiefs and warriors, turned out to help, and all worked from one field to another until all the seed was in the ground. While they planted, they were entertained by storytellers, singers, and musicians performing on deerskin drums.

The fields were then constantly guarded. Old women watched from high scaffoldings by day, frightening marauding birds away.

The Creeks also raised what the Spaniards called small dogs that did not bark, which were probably domesticated opossums. The Spaniards thought they made "good eating." Game was especially common in the southern states, with plenty of deer, bear, squirrels, rabbits, waterfowl, and turkeys. The streams were full of fish, though with so much game about many of the southern Indians fished for sport rather than for food.

They shot fish with arrows; speared them with stalks of cane, which were strong enough to bring up fish two feet long; caught them in

long stone weirs, ending in fish-trap baskets. Some Indians caught the
big southern catfish by diving into the water, with something red for
bait. As the "cat" tried to swallow the flash of color, the fisherman
grasped the fish, dragged it to the surface and ashore. This could not
have been the huge Mississippi River catfish, which grew to weigh
one and two hundred pounds in those days. Sometimes the Chickasaws and other tribes formed lines of men who swam under water,
holding hand nets in front of them. The trouble with this method was
that it brought in about as many watersnakes as fish.

Passing through the country in the springtime, De Soto and his men
saw our prehistoric South at its best. They found along the trails
countless roses, growing wild, and thought they were like the roses of
Spain. They admired the fine forests, the fertile fields, the rich dress
of the natives. They were impressed by the good wild strawberries—
better, they thought, than their own European variety. The plants
grew in such a thickness as we could not even imagine today. One
later traveler said that large-sized strawberries covered the ground as
with a red cloth. There were wild potatoes, wild greens and herbs.
The Spaniards were lucky in not eating the wrong thing. There is not
much poisonous vegetation in North America, though one early explorer thought he lost a few men because they had eaten the wrong
herbs. Newcomers soon learned to avoid eating fruits and other vegetation that were not eaten by birds or beasts.

The Spaniards liked the hickory milk called "powhicora," a drink
popular among the southern Indians. Squaws pounded acorns, hickory nuts, walnuts, and probably pecans, which they dropped, shell and
all, into water. The fragments of shell sank to the bottom, after which
the thick, white, oily milk was skimmed off and eaten with cornbread,
hot from the fire. It was also used as a "thin drink," mixed with corn-
meal, or flavored to taste with ashes of burnt straw. Ashes of various
kinds were a flavoring much enjoyed by eastern and southern Indians.

Thus far, De Soto had not been doing badly, though he had not, to
be sure, found any golden empires to plunder. Clearly this land, however fertile, was neither another Mexico nor another Peru; and, since
De Soto longed to be another Cortez or Pizarro, he kept moving on.
There had been no sign of anything like treasure, except fresh-water

pearls, taken from river mussels. There were plenty of these. The woman chief of Cofitachequi—who ruled the Indians on the South Carolina and Georgia sides of the Savannah River, around Augusta— gave De Soto a whole necklace of them.

Robbing a tomb, the Spaniards found corpses decorated all over with pearls. They collected about two hundred pounds of them; but they were valueless in Europe, where people knew what real jewels were. When the grave robbers found something green like an emerald, there was much excitement—until they realized that it was just glass, and European glass at that! Near the green bit of glass, they found other glass beads, rosaries, and iron axes—remnants of Ayllón's disastrous expedition thirteen years before!

Even if there were no treasure, the Spaniards found this a good country. Some wanted to stay forever. A few slipped away, deserting their fellows, and would not return to the expedition. Indian life and Indian girls were more attractive than De Soto's endless marching. The life of the Indians also appealed strongly to the Negro slaves with the expedition. Some of them stole away into the forests, to spend the rest of their lives in this new, free land.

But De Soto would not be content till he found gold. Most of the other Spaniards had the same dreams of wealth to urge them on. From central Florida north through Georgia, cutting across western South Carolina, that strange column of Spanish horsemen, with their slaves and pigs following, wound in a long, single file, along the narrow forest trails. With swords and lances and armor gleaming, they struggled on, until they came at last through a lofty range of mountains—probably the Great Smokies or the southern end of the Blue Ridge. Crossing a corner of North Carolina and a corner of Tennessee, they turned south again through Alabama into Mississippi.

As De Soto passed, most Indian villages sent out carrying parties to meet him and help him with his baggage. It was no doubt their polite way of hurrying these not-too-welcome white strangers on their way, and getting rid of them. Once a chief gave them a guide who had private instructions to take them some place—any place—where they would starve to death.

Though there were deserters from the expedition, there were also some additions. One chief gave De Soto his daughter, "a fine young girl." Other chiefs made him presents of their sisters or one or two of their squaws. Sometimes the soldiers could buy Indian squaws in exchange for mirrors and knives. As time went on, the appearance of that extraordinary march began to change. The gleaming weapons grew rusty. The number of pigs increased, as did the number of Indian baggage bearers and Indian prisoners, in chains. Then, gradually, more and more Indian girls and squaws began to join the column.

Reaching central Alabama, De Soto was met outside one town by a chief, carried on a litter borne on the shoulders of his principal men. He was seated on a cushion and covered with a mantle of marten skins. On his head he wore a diadem of plumes, and he was surrounded by flute players.

De Soto found the country here to be thickly settled with numerous large towns, and fields full of corn and beans extending from one town to another. In this pleasant country he rested for a month. Then he pushed farther into Alabama, till he reached the Creek village of Mauvilla, where he quarreled with the chief. There had been very little fighting, up to this point: but now De Soto had a real battle. He won it, but not before twenty of his men were killed and 250 wounded. In the end he burned the offending village and drove the Creeks away, killing 2,500 of them. His own losses included all his medicines, the pearls, and much other baggage. With no medicine left, they dressed the wounds of the injured with the fat of dead Indians.

At this critical moment, word reached De Soto—by native runners, who carried news swiftly from village to village—that his ships were only six days' march away, on the Gulf Coast. But the news came at the wrong time. More than a year of exploration had produced no treasure, except his stock of pearls—and they had just been lost. Worse, he had lost over a hundred men from wounds and sickness and had absolutely nothing to show for it. Ashamed of his failure thus far, he decided to send no news of himself to the ships, until he should have discovered a rich country.

The Spaniards amused themselves by burning over the country around Mauvilla, where the fight had taken place, and then rested there about a month longer, before pushing on into Mississippi. After a two weeks' march through unbroken forest, they came to Chicaca, a Chickasaw village of some twenty lodges, near the modern town of Redland. Here was more fertile country. The corn crop was in, and De Soto soon had supplies for the winter. The local chief gave the Spaniards 150 rabbits, Indian shawls, and leather clothing, which— after their losses at Mauvilla—they must have sorely needed. De Soto introduced the Chickasaws to pork, of which they became so fond that there was an epidemic of pig stealing from "some houses where the hogs slept." De Soto put an end to this, characteristically, by having two thieves shot with arrows and a third sent back to his home with both hands cut off.

At first everything seemed peaceful in this Chickasaw country, and the Spaniards rested here about two months. De Soto made many such long halts. No doubt, he had to do this to give his pigs a chance to fatten and raise their little ones.

As his rest period ended and he prepared to move on, De Soto asked the Chickasaws for two hundred bearers. When they seemed reluctant, he prepared for trouble none too soon. Early one morning in March, 1541, the Spanish camp was attacked from four different directions. The town was soon in a blaze. The Spaniards, waking in confusion, could not find their weapons or their mounts. In the end, the Indians were frightened off by terrified horses, which had gotten loose and were charging about frantically in the darkness.

When daylight came, the Spaniards took stock of the situation, and found many of the soldiers naked, their clothing having been burned. Weapons and saddles had been lost. Some horses had burned to death. Only one hundred pigs were left of the large drove they had had when they arrived two months earlier. Stark naked, men huddled about large fires. They would have made perfect targets for prowling Indian archers; but the warriors had disappeared. The Spaniards wrapped themselves in mats which they made out of dried grass sewed together. They made such funny looking soldiers, that their comrades laughed at them.

No disaster, however, could stop De Soto. He set up a forge and put his blacksmith to work repairing damages to their weapons. When a new attack came, he was ready for it, and beat the Indians off. By the end of April, he was on his way again, through unending forests in the almost uninhabited northwest corner of Mississippi. They came to pondy places in the woods, little lakes they had to cross. Sometimes they had to swim. The change in the country showed that they were approaching a great river. They struck the Mississippi first at a village called Quizquiz, just south of the Tennessee border.

Exhausted and hungry, De Soto and his men wanted peace. Fortunately for them, the Indians wanted no trouble, either. The appearance of the Spaniards filled them with foreboding. A legend handed down from their ancestors prophesied that the tribe would some day be conquered by a white race. White men had now come! The Indians did not feel very confident or happy.

Standing at a point somewhere near either Council Bend or Walnut Bend, in Mississippi, some distance south of Memphis, Tennessee, the leader decided to build boats and cross the river. It did not look as if it would be easy. They had reached the Mississippi during the spring floods. The water was muddy, swift, and very deep. The river was so wide that a man, standing on the far shore, "could not be told, whether he were a man or something else."

While the expedition was still on the eastern bank, they saw, one day, an astonishing sight. Two hundred canoes were coming toward them, across the great river. It was an impressive fleet. Each canoe was filled with brightly painted warriors, carrying shields ornamented with feathers. Their beads glistened in the sunlight. On their heads they wore great bunches of white and colored plumes.

Wicker shields protected the men at the paddles. Warriors stood in line from bow to stern of each craft, with arrows ready to let fly. The canoes were heavy, stable river dugouts, quite unlike the light and "tippy" bark craft of Northern Lake Indians.

In the flagship of this fighting fleet, under an awning, sat the chief, giving orders to lesser chiefs, also sitting under awnings in their own canoes. The Indians had come out to show the white strangers what force they had, if it came to a fight. Nevertheless, they approached in a friendly way and brought with them barges loaded with presents of fish and bread, made of persimmon pulp. When the Spaniards, suspecting a trick, shot their crossbows, the Indians withdrew, but there was no fighting.

Since these Indians did not seem dangerous, De Soto and his men stayed in this region a month, building boats. Still, he was taking no chances. When they had finished, De Soto sent a protecting guard with the first landing party. After this, the boats went back and forth until the whole force, including the pigs, was safely ferried over. The boats were then knocked to pieces to save the iron spikes.

In Arkansas, there was more hard going through swamps and bayous, and around endless river bends. All one day, until sunset, they marched through water, sometimes up to their knees, in places up to their waists. This was the worst region for swamp and water they had encountered. Even Indians did not live on the marshy river borders.

Finally they came to higher and dryer level land. There they found nut trees, probably pecans, as well as mulberry and persimmon trees. Indian villages began to dot the countryside so thickly the Spaniards could often see several settlements at once. These Indians wore woven shawls, and their shields were of raw buffalo hide that the Spaniards called cowhide.

De Soto's men had not yet seen our buffalo, but they were soon to learn of them, for while resting here where food was plentiful and fish were abundant, De Soto sent a scouting party to explore to the north. It came back with the news that there were few people but innumerable animals, which they described as "cattle." The Indians, in that country, they told their leader, lived upon the meat of these "cattle." It is evident that De Soto's scouts had reached the buffalo plains.

This was the first report that reached white men of the teeming herds on the prairies, though Coronado's expedition, farther west, would soon be passing through the buffalo country. De Soto himself saw only the buffalo robes the Indians were using. These, as one of his officers said, made good bed covers, because they were soft and warm and covered with thick wool. Most of this band of Spaniards never went far enough north to see the great animals. Even those who did, saw only a few. The really immense herds were at that season farther north. Probably De Soto never understood, even from his scouts' report, that there could possibly be enough of the creatures to provide meat for all his force. It did not matter much. De Soto still had those much-traveled pigs of his, to fall back on as a meat reserve. What he wanted now was corn. He turned west to get it.

As the column pushed into what now is Arkansas, the country at first was fertile and level. Halfway to what is now Little Rock, however, they began to find immense tangled thickets, growing around ponds, shallow pools, and winding bayous. It was very picturesque but it did not appeal to the splashing, floundering soldiers. There was only one comfort. However bad the traveling, Arkansas provided easy food. Fish were so plentiful that these early Arkansas travelers did not use hooks or lines or nets. They merely clubbed as many fish as they happened to want for dinner.

As the winter of 1541 drew on, De Soto's determination waned. He was ready to give up. Somewhere near present-day Fort Smith, Arkansas, he passed across the Oklahoma border, and then turned eastward, seeking a way to the sea, where he hoped to build ships. For the first three winter months he camped in Arkansas, where his men ate corn, beans, walnuts, dried persimmons, and rabbits, which Indians taught them to snare. In the spring they moved near Arkansas Post, on the Arkansas River, close to the Mississippi. De Soto marched south to the vicinity of what is now Arkansas City. Here he found it would be impossible to march on, overland to the Gulf of Mexico. Canebrakes were too frequent, scrubby thickets blocked too much of the country. There were also "great bogs that came out of the river." This part of the Mississippi Valley seemed entirely uninhabited—and no wonder!

It was clear at last that after all their searching, hardships, and danger, De Soto and his men would never find cities filled with gold and jewels. Realizing that his dream was gone, his efforts all in vain, De Soto became despondent. He gave up, in spirit; and when he did that, the physical strength went out of him. Or, perhaps, his courage failed as his physique gave out. Somewhere on the bank of the Mississippi, no one knows just where, he died. To keep the Indians from knowing they had lost their leader, his men sank the body in the river.

One of the officers, Luis de Moscoso, took over the command. At first he led them, through terrific heat, southwest into Texas, but they found only scrub and forest. Journeying back across Arkansas, they camped in timbered country. Here there was better wood for ship building than they had seen in all of "Florida"—by which the Spaniards meant most of the southern United States. Axes began to ring.

In June, 1543, a year and a month after De Soto's death, 311 bedraggled men, who had survived those four hard years of travel in the primitive wilderness, floated down the Arkansas River in their crudely made boats. On down the Mississippi they went, out into the Gulf, to Mexico at last—and safety.

None of them ever guessed that he had passed close to country which really did produce a little gold. Later explorers along the Florida, Georgia, and South Carolina coast found some among the natives.

In spite of all the courage of the men and De Soto's skilled leadership, his venture was the most spectacular of Spanish failures. It brought death to the leader, death to half his followers. It discovered no empires, it brought home no gold. It found no treasure save some worthless river pearls—and it lost most of these. But except for the march of Coronado, it was the most complete and far-reaching exploration of North America that had yet been undertaken.

CHAPTER 6

Coronado in Kansas

1540–1542

THE RETURN of Cabeza de Vaca aroused as much interest in Mexico as it did in Spain. While De Soto was exploring the southern part of our country, Cabeza de Vaca was telling his stories to the Spanish viceroy and other Spaniards who were living in Mexico. Don Antonio de Mendoza, the viceroy, was as eager to hear these tales as Cabeza de Vaca was to tell them.

The story that impressed his hearers most was the one Indians had told Cabeza about the Seven Cities of Cíbola. It was true, Cabeza admitted, that he had not seen anything of the sort himself. But he had heard accounts of large and powerful cities in the Southwest, with buildings four and five stories high. No doubt these sounded like skyscrapers to the Spaniards four hundred years ago. In reality, these were only the many-floored adobe pueblos of Arizona and New Mexico. But to other Indians, living in huts or tepees, they seemed impressive.

When Cabeza de Vaca and the other Spaniards heard about "cities," they thought at once of the great cities of Europe, or of the Aztec cities of Mexico. The word as used by the red men did not mean the same thing, therefore, as it did to white men, but neither group knew that.

The viceroy passed the news of these Seven Cities on to one of his provincial governors, Francisco Vásquez de Coronado, who would lead an expedition to find the fabulous cities.

The obvious thing to do first was to send Cabeza de Vaca ahead to look over the country, since he had already been in the mysterious land to the north. But Cabeza would not go; he had had enough exploring. There was the Negro, Estebánico, and he was a slave. He could be sent wherever his master wished. Mendoza bought him and sent him ahead with Brother Marcos de Niza, to reconnoiter for the expedition Coronado was to lead.

Estebánico seems to have been delighted with the arrangement, especially as he preceded Brother Marcos by several days' journey. In Mexico he was a slave. But in the wilderness he was an independent and important person—familiar to the Indians, among whom he had traveled with Cabeza de Vaca, a powerful medicine man, known to have effected remarkable cures. Moreover, the Negro's dark skin was much admired by the Indians.

Troubles soon arose, however. Estebánico was easily spoiled by the Indians' admiration, by their gifts, and by their flattery. It was not long until Estebánico was keeping for himself the turquoises he collected from the Indians, instead of handing them over to Brother Marcos.

Estebánico was supposed to send back to Brother Marcos reports on what he was seeing. Since Estebánico could not write, he could not send written messages. Neither could he send oral messages by Indian runners. They would soon have learned that the newcomers were seeking treasure; and of course, language was a problem. Brother Marcos found an ingenious code: He told the Negro to send back by Indian runners, wooden crosses, which could easily be formed from branches. A little cross nine inches long meant that whatever Estebánico found, in the land or villages he passed, was only moderate— yielding no more than the usual Indian presents. If he thought he had made an important discovery, he was to send back a cross twice as long. If he found a land better than Mexico itself, he was to send a very large cross.

Unfortunately good land did not mean the same thing to Estebánico and Brother Marcos. Brother Marcos, thinking of his leader Coronado, was looking for thickly inhabited country where the people had amassed wealth, in other words, cities. But Estebánico, who had always been a slave, thought any country was good where he was having a good time. And the nicer the Indians were to him, the better time he had. He sent back two crosses that were as high as a man.

Brother Marcos devoutly gave thanks to God and hurried forward, encouraged by still a third large cross that Estebánico had left by the way. Passing through a valley that was settled by attractive and peaceful Indians, and so bountiful in food that it could feed more than three hundred men and horses, Brother Marcos thought they were now on the right track. It was not a rich country yet, but Brother Marcos himself saw Indians wearing turquois necklaces with five and six loops. No gold so far but surely they were getting warmer.

Suddenly, like a dash of cold water, came bad news.

Estebánico was dead. Indians had killed him.

The story has been pieced together from ancient accounts that Zuñi tradition handed from father to son for many generations. This is what happened:

The slave had begun to put on too many airs. He had pretended to be a mighty medicine man. Remembering how Cabeza de Vaca had "cured" Indians' headaches by making the sign of the Cross over them, Estebánico tried to claim magic power himself. To impress the Indians, he began to wear feathers, trying to look more important than their own chiefs. He wore magic rattles on his ankles and wrists, and carried the magic gourd rattle of the medicine man, adorned with strings of bells, and two feathers, one white and one red. He enticed young girls to follow him, which naturally aroused jealousy among the Indian boys. Other attendants brought the Negro's escort up to three hundred Indians—and a dog. By this time he was laden with a large number of turquoises which the natives had given him. Many Indians were awed by him.

Thus, in ceremony and state, Estebánico triumphantly approached the first "City of Cíbola." It was the flourishing pueblo of Hawikuh, which is now a heap of ruins.

Copying manners he had seen practiced by his own masters, Estebánico sent a messenger forward, bearing his magic gourd rattle. The Negro, in all his finery, followed by a retinue of three hundred people, stretching behind him on the march, must have looked like a conquering hero, coming across the desert.

The Zuñis did not like what they saw.

A chief of Hawikuh took the gourd from the messenger, dashed it angrily to the ground, and told him to get out. If Estebánico and his train entered his village, said the chief, he would kill them all.

But by this time, Estebánico had become foolishly spoiled and cocksure. He simply turned the threat aside, saying only that when people showed anger at first, they later received him better. On he went toward the pueblo. When warriors, coming out to meet him, told him not to try to enter, he made his next mistake. He demanded that they give him turquoises and women. Estebánico had now gone a great deal too far. The warriors seized him. They took away his turquoises and a great many other things he had obtained from Indians along the way. When they had taken everything, they shut him up in a hut outside the pueblo and gave him no food.

Early one morning, Estebánico was allowed to leave his hut for a little while. He and some of the Indian guides who had come with him made the mistake of trying to escape. A shower of arrows from the bows of Hawikuh warriors filled the air behind them. That was the end of Estebánico.

When news of the Negro's death reached Brother Marcos, he turned around and, after giving away everything he had, except his priestly vestments, to pacify his own Indians, he started for Mexico as fast as he could go.

When Brother Marcos got home, he, too, was full of stories. He did not say he had seen gold, but that he had heard about it. He described a certain valley: "I was told that there is much gold there and that the natives make it into vessels and jewels for their ears, and into little blades with which to wipe away their sweat."

After Brother Marcos visited a barbershop—a place where people still are likely to talk too much—the stories grew taller as they spread from mouth to mouth. It was not long before the report was going around that there was more gold to be found in this new country, than had been found in all Peru!

Now it was Coronado's turn to march north from Mexico. In January of 1540 he was commissioned to lead the expedition to the Seven Cities of Cíbola. By the end of February his army was ready, with about three hundred Spaniards, a large number of slaves, one thousand horses, and several hundred pack animals. Like De Soto, Coronado drove live stock along to provide meat on the way. In addition, he had about thirteen hundred friendly Indians. Brother Marcos went along as guide.

Coronado himself glittered in gilded armor; his helmet was adorned with plumes. Eleven soldiers wore full armor. About forty had chain mail. The rest wore stout leather coats. Their weapons included swords, daggers, lances, and native weapons. Nineteen soldiers carried crossbows, and twenty-seven had arquebuses. The arquebus was the sixteenth-century shoulder firearm—the predecessor of the musket. A column such as this moving into the southwestern desert must have looked most impressive and truly threatening to the Indians who watched its approach.

There was even more to the expedition than this host of white men, Indians, Negro slaves, and animals. For while Coronado was marching north through Mexico and into Arizona, Spanish ships under the naval officer, Pedro de Alarcón, sailed up the Gulf of California to support the land army. The Spaniards tried to think of everything. But alas, nobody knew then that Lower California, which they thought was an island, was really a peninsula which would cut Alarcón's ships off from the Pacific Ocean. Nor did any one know that part of the highest mountain range in our whole country lay between the west coast and the country Coronado was to explore.

The expedition entered the territory of what is today the United States, through the San Pedro Valley. This runs north from the modern Mexican border, through eastern Arizona, till it reaches the Gila River, not far from the Coolidge Dam. They went up the Gila to an old pueblo which the Aztecs called Chichilti-calli, or Red House, because it was built of red earth. After the glowing reports they had heard, Chichilti-calli was a terrible disappointment to the Spaniards. They were disgusted to find it a mere ruin, uninhabited and solitary. It did look as if, once upon a time, it had been an Indian fortress.

They had already encountered the Rocky Mountain goats and now began to see cougars and wildcats. They passed through territory where prickly pears and cactus grew and advanced into Pueblo country.

An even greater shock awaited the expedition when they first saw an inhabited pueblo. Here was no splended city gleaming with gold, silver, and jewels. The pueblo was only a group of Indian dwellings made of clay and mud. Brother Marcos was reviled and cursed by many of the others for having led them to expect so much. The friar may have been encouraged by his government to exaggerate a bit—it was good propaganda to get men to go on the expedition. But Coronado himself was disturbed when he saw how wild popular rumor had exaggerated Brother Marco's statements.

One of the strangest things about North America in those early days was the astonishing speed with which news got around. The Indians could tell Alarcón about Coronado, and Coronado about Alarcón, though their routes were far apart. While Coronado was marching across desert and prairie, De Soto was marching across the southeastern states, far enough west to get some distance inside Texas. In spite of the wide span between them, Coronado's men picked up news of De Soto. It was about that time that word of Coronado reached an explorer named Juan de Cabrillo who was then examining the California coast. An Indian told Cabrillo of eleven Christians who were traveling about a week's journey inland. The Indians had their own ways of spreading news quickly. Similarly, Coronado now learned that Indians had seen Alarcón's ships in the Gulf of California, but it was evident that at such a distance they would be of no help to his army.

Still hopeful, he moved on into the uninhabited desert somewhere along the southern part of the Arizona-New Mexico boundary. For several days they found no grass whatever for their horses. At last they came thankfully to a cool river and grass that was like the grass of Spain. There were also nut and mulberry trees.

Coronado's route north then brought him to Hawikuh, a pueblo near the modern American town of Ojo Caliente, New Mexico.

The Zuñis, who had killed Estebánico here, were still hostile. They attacked before Coronado was in sight of their city, but were beaten off. That night, Zuñi signal fires flared and were answered by others. Coronado observed that these Indians' method of communication was as good as the Spaniards themselves could have devised. The next day he pushed on to their village, for his food was almost exhausted. He sent a small party forward to make peace, if possible. But they were answered with arrows. Then Coronado and his troops arrived to find the Indians drawn up on the plain. When the Spaniards did not attack, the Indians closed in with showers of arrows, until a Spanish charge drove them back to their pueblo. The Zuñis now fought from their flat rooftops, hurling down many great stones. Coronado's elaborate gilt armor made him a chief target. He was hit in the foot with an arrow and twice knocked down with stones. But the Spaniards proved too strong for the Zuñis, and in the end they secured Hawikuh with its large store of corn, while the Zuñis themselves fled to their stronghold on Thunder Mountain.

There was an attractive modesty about Coronado. He wrote to the viceroy Mendoza: "The Indians all directed their attack against me because my armor was gilded and glittering, and on this account I was hurt more than the rest, and not because I had done more or was farther in advance than the others; for all these gentlemen and soldiers bore themselves well, as was expected of them."

With the victory came more disillusionment, however. There was no gold or silver here, either. The cities the Spaniards had expected to find were only little settlements. There was plenty of corn and some turkeys.

Just where the explorer was, he had no very clear idea. He thought (as he wrote down) that he was nearer the Pacific than the Atlantic Ocean, and in this, of course, he was right. He thought the Arctic Ocean must be much farther away, and he was right about that, too. But he did not know that he was near the Great Continental Divide;

he did not even know there existed such a height of land. He did not know that, at one point, he was only fifty miles west of the Petrified Forest. He did not know that a little farther north lay the amazing and, even then, ancient ruins of the Chaco Canyon, great buildings and canals, where red men long centuries before had built up an isolated, peaceful civilization and then, one day, sealing their houses, had vanished, no man knows where or why. The Grand Canyon of the Colorado lay about two hundred miles to the northwest. He did not see that, either, but a reconnoitering party of about a dozen men set out to find a large river about which they had been told and which was, in fact, the Colorado. At the end of twenty days' journey, across Arizona desert in midsummer, when their supply of water was very low, they found themselves looking down—far, far down—into a tremendous canyon. There lay the Colorado River, in plain sight, but they could not reach it.

For three days they tried to find a way down the jagged, rocky canyon wall. Each time, they failed. Then, at last, some one found a place that looked promising, and three adventurers started the long climb. Eagerly their companions watched the scrambling figures grow smaller and smaller as they swung slowly into the abyss, toward the water far below. On they went, on and on, until at last they were lost from the sight of those waiting on the rim. There was a long, anxious pause. Then, in the afternoon, tiny distant figures could be seen again, scrambling upward from rock to rock. About four o'clock they swung their legs over the canyon's rim.

No water! It had been another failure.

There were too many obstacles in the way of their reaching the canyon's bottom. They had gone only about one third of the distance. The men who stayed on the canyon's rim, thought they saw boulders far below, which seemed to be as high as a man, but those who had gone down reported that they were taller "than the great tower of Seville," the 295-foot bell tower of Seville Cathedral, in Spain.

Their Indian guides warned the reconnoitering party there would be no water in the country ahead, for three or four days travel. The Indians themselves could cross that country only by leaving gourds of water buried in the ground along the trail. The Spaniards, already short, had to turn back, regretfully, to Hawikuh. Behind them, the Grand Canyon lay in majestic peace. No other white men came to see it for two hundred years.

Another patrol discovered the lower part of the Colorado River, and found letters buried there by the naval commander, Alarcón, before he turned back downstream.

While Coronado was marching inland, Alarcón had gone to the end of the Gulf of California and then, in small boats, he and some of his men went some distance up the Colorado River. He saw land that was to be called California, but he could not find Coronado's army. In the end, he left his buried messages for Coronado's men to find, turned around, and went back.

Coronado and his men continued to explore. Since they could not cover the entire country themselves, they questioned friendly Indians. They were astonished by the pueblo at Ácoma, New Mexico, perched atop the high mesa. This was the home of the Keresan Indians, who are still living there. Ácoma is the oldest structure in the whole United States that has been continually occupied by human beings.

The only way to reach this lofty home was by a stairway, carved out of the rock itself—about two hundred steps, then a narrower staircase. Beyond that there was a still further climb, which had to be made by small holes in the cliff, where the Indians held on with fingers and toes alone. The Spaniards, hardly able to make their way up this last stretch, watched with amazement the ease with which the Indians of Ácoma went up and down. They moved "so freely that they carry loads of provisions, and the women carry water, and they do not seem to touch the walls with their hands."

Thus far, Coronado had met only various Pueblo Indians. After exploring part of Arizona and marching clear across New Mexico, he had his first meeting with plains Indians near the New Mexico-Texas border. These Indians were entirely different from any the Spaniards had seen. Coronado calls them "Querechos." They were probably Apaches or Tonkawas.

They reminded the Spaniards of wandering Arab tribes, always moving, dwelling only in tents.

Their tents, the Spaniards said, were made of the dressed skins of "cattle." They were really buffalo hide tepees, for these Indians were plains wanderers, depending wholly on the great herds of buffalo for most of their livelihood. They had no fixed homes or villages, nor did they cultivate the land. They made their tepees, their clothing, and their moccasins of buffalo hide. Buffalo robes served them for bedding. Buffalo meat was their principal food, though of course they sometimes killed other animals.

From buffalo sinews, they made thread with which to sew their clothes and ropes with which to fasten their tents. From buffalo bones they shaped awls and other tools. The bladders they used as water containers. They used buffalo dung for firewood, since no trees grew on the great grass prairie lands. To those wandering plains tribes the buffalo was everything, the entire means of existence; food, clothing, shelter, fuel. It is no wonder that, after the white man moved into the West and killed off the great herds, the plains tribes became weak. They had lost their way of living.

The Spaniards knew that this strange American animal existed, even before they saw it. While they were still among the Pueblos, unknown Indians had come to see the white newcomers. They had brought with them presents of buffalo robes, buffalo hide shields, and buffalo-horn headgear. The buffalo hides interested the Spaniards exceedingly, and puzzled them, too, for they could not imagine what kind of animal they came from. Explanations by the visiting Indians were not much use. Finally the Spaniards decided that the animals "seemed to be cows, although from the hides this did not seem possible, because the hair was woolly and snarled."

The Spaniards watched with great interest when, for the first time, they saw a village of plains Indians preparing to move on to new buffalo hunting grounds. They had no horses, as yet. The only horses in all North America were those the white men had brought with them. Plains Indians used dogs to carry their belongings. They loaded them like pack mules, with little pads, packsaddles, and girths. If the loads slipped, the dogs had been taught to howl for some one to come and straighten them.

In later centuries, horses began to go astray on the prairies, though it is doubtful if any of these came from the Coronado expedition. These stray horses soon multiplied and became the wild mustangs of our western prairies. These grassy western plains were a horse's paradise, with plenty of food and room to outrun their enemies. In time, the plains Indians learned to catch these wild horses, or steal white men's. With horses to ride, they became more powerful than the tribes who had to hunt, travel, and fight on foot.

In Coronado's time, however, the Indians north of Mexico had never seen horses, just as the white men had never seen buffalo. If the white men were astonished at the huge "cattle" of the prairies, the Indians were even more astonished at animals large enough for men to ride. At first they had strange ideas. Some supposed that horse and rider were a single creature—a kind of centaur. The Pueblos believed that horses killed and ate Indians. Father Kino, the missionary priest who traveled through Arizona country 150 years after Coronado, found that little Indian boys were glad to gather grass for his horses, being happy to find that horses ate grass instead of little boys.

Coronado's troubles increased as soon as he moved out on the vast trackless plains. It was often impossible to tell direction, for the Spaniards were exploring in the days before pocket compasses had been invented. The compass of those days was used on ships alone. Unless there were occasional small villages of Indian tepees, this flat country had no landmarks at all. There were no hills, no streams, no trees, no bushes, not even stones. Just grass. The abundant grass the buffalo ate. Grass as far as the eye could see.

There was no way to find directions, because all directions looked the same. Men got lost. Sometimes those who wandered away from the moving column had to wait for the sun to go down, before they could tell east from west. It was almost impossible to follow the trail of their own column. The short grass did not remain trampled. It sprang upright again, almost at once. It was impossible to see where horses had trodden.

When men were missing, guns banged, horns blew, and bonfires blazed to guide them in to camp. Some men found their way back after two or three days. Some never found it.

When they came at last to the first great herds of buffalo, their horses shied violently at the strange sight and smell of the huge beasts.

Then, when the buffalo themselves took fright, the astonished explorers were horrified at the crazy fury of a stampede. Once they saw a whole herd dash toward a ravine into which the animals fell till it was filled up. Then other buffalo rushed across, trampling the bodies. Men following on horseback fell on top of the buffalo, not knowing what had happened. Three of the horses disappeared among the struggling, frightened buffalo and were never recovered.

Equally fearsome was the Spaniards' first experience of a prairie mid-summer hailstorm—a "whirl wind" which caught them resting in a ravine. The hail came down with such violence that it tore tents to pieces and dented helmets. The hailstones were as large as bowls and even larger, Coronado wrote, and as thick as raindrops. They bruised and terrified the horses. All except three (which men happened to be holding) stampeded. Coronado might have lost them entirely, but a fortunate accident saved them. When the storm struck, the horses happened to be in a ravine, where they could not scatter, as they would have on the open prairie.

Coronado's men moved north across part of Oklahoma and halfway into Kansas. They traversed strange and wonderful country. They saw animals they never had seen before. They met strange peoples with strange ways of living. In amazement they watched Indians shoot the great buffalo with bows and arrows.

In Kansas they saw round huts thatched with grass, woven tightly and overlapping, so that they were warm and waterproof. These were the homes of the Wichita Indians. We know where the Spaniards were at this time mainly because they described the peculiar Wichita shelters.

But, in spite of all the wonders they encountered, of gold and silver there was not a trace. Coronado seemed to find everything but what he came to find.

By the time he reached central Kansas, Coronado had traveled 2,500 miles from Mexico—a figure that can be depended on, for certain infantrymen had been specially detailed to trudge along, counting their paces, all the way. Here, at last, he gave up hope and turned back to Mexico, his dreams of treasure completely gone.

CHAPTER 7

Cartier Comes to Canada

1534–1535

WHILE Cabeza de Vaca and his companions were struggling, half starved, along the Gulf coast toward Mexico and safety, two little French ships were approaching America, far to the north, on the top side of the continent. Hardly bigger than modern yachts, the two together carried only about sixty sailors. But, small as they were, the little craft were under a bold commander, whose skillful navigation had brought them safely across the stormy North Atlantic. Now they were nosing cautiously south, along the unknown coast of Newfoundland. The commander was Jacques Cartier.

Nobody knows much about this Frenchman's early life. He was born in 1491, in the Brittany town, St. Malo, and so belonged to the hardy, seafaring Breton race. He became the first of many great French explorers in North America. His little ships began the adventurous series of exploration along the St. Lawrence River that were to give France control of eastern Canada. From this foothold, through the next two hundred years, other Frenchmen with all of Cartier's own boldness and daring, were to carry exploration north, south, and west, deep into the heart of the continent.

As they drew in toward North America, but before they had even seen its coast, Cartier's ships passed a lonely island. Now called Funk Island, it rises from the sea, in a single mass of rock. On it swarmed more sea birds than any of the amazed Frenchmen had ever imagined. "All of the ships of France might load a cargo of them without once perceiving that any had been removed," said Cartier. In the air there were "an hundred times as many more as on the island itself." A visiting French Jesuit father, a few years later, was nearly knocked down because so many frightened birds flew violently against him.

When Cartier's Frenchmen came closer, they saw large black and white fowl, as big as geese, settled among the rocks or swimming along shore. These had wings so small they could not possibly fly. They were the great auks, birds we shall never see, for they were completely killed off about a hundred years ago.

Tired of salt meat, which had been their main diet all the long voyage from France, the sailors went ashore, eyeing the fat birds hungrily. Within half an hour they had loaded their ships with fresh meat. Since Indians did not paddle their canoes so far out, the birds had probably never seen a human. Being unafraid, they were easy to catch. The hungry crews feasted on fresh poultry; and each ship salted down four or five barrels for future use.

Another surprise was a polar bear, the first these Frenchmen had ever seen, and probably the first one any white men had ever seen. Apparently the bear, too, had come to dine on birds and birds' eggs. The sailors tried in vain to catch the huge animal. Next day, as the ships sailed in toward the coast, they saw the big bear swimming desperately for shore. This time they killed him and feasted on bear meat, which they thought was as good as beef. Probably it wasn't, but after weeks of eating salt meat at sea, any fresh meat seemed delicious.

Sailing up the Newfoundland coast, past its tip, and steering thence southwest, Cartier and his sixty men found the Gulf of St. Lawrence opening out before them, revealing another bird island, now called Greenly Island. Here, too, there were immense numbers of birds. For the first time the white men saw red-beaked puffins, queer creatures that burrow into the earth to make their nests under flat rocks. The steep sides of that same island are even today perforated with their burrows. There were also eider ducks, whose eggs the men collected.

Cartier was the first to leave a record of these waters, though not the first white man to visit them, as he himself soon found out. The very next day his ships met a large fishing vessel from La Rochelle. Cartier now learned that Frenchmen, as well as Basques from the north coast of Spain or the extreme south of France, had been fishing there for at least thirty years. Perhaps they had been doing so before Columbus; but, if so, as most fishermen do, they had kept their choicest fishing spots a secret.

Feeling their way cautiously, Cartier and his men kept taking constant soundings, to find the depth of these unknown waters. It would never do to run aground on rocks that might lie just under the surface near this rocky shore line. Nowadays, waterways and shore lines are carefully charted and marked with lighthouses and warning buoys to show danger spots to navigators. The early explorers had no such aids; and, if they damaged their ships badly, there was no way to repair them.

Slowly, Cartier's two little ships crept along the west coast of Newfoundland. The men were delighted to be able to catch a hundred codfish in an hour. They saw still more rocky islands, filled with birds. These are now called Bird Rocks. Cartier said they were as completely covered with birds as a field with grass. On Great Bird Rock, nests almost touched each other. These birds were gannets.

At first, Cartier's Frenchmen had been horrified by the barren, rocky shores of Newfoundland. Here was nothing but stones and rocks, with a little sour earth, in which grew only moss and stunted shrubs. So grim was the impression this savage landscape produced, that Cartier wondered whether it might not be "the land God gave to Cain." But, the land began to improve when the explorers approached the rich meadowland of the St. Lawrence River. Landing on Bryan Island, in the middle of the Bay, they found it covered with fine trees and meadows, fields of wild "oats," and "pease" in flower. There were also wild roses, strawberries, and fragrant herbs. This was a sharp contrast to the rocky coast and islands they had been seeing.

In astonishment, they beheld walruses for the first time. Not knowing what the strange creatures were, Cartier tried to describe them—"great beasts like large oxen, which have two tusks in the jaws like elephants' tusks and swim about in the water." His sailors tried to catch one they found asleep on the shore; but, as they drew near, the "sea ox" threw himself into the water.

As Cartier and his men cruised around the Gulf, they encountered more of the giant, tusked creatures. There were also huge whales and other small white whales, called belugas. All these animals, like the polar bears, have long since vanished from the St. Lawrence—driven back into the north by the white man's powerful weapons.

Coasting along Prince Edward Island, the French explorer was so impressed by the primeval forest, that he landed four times, just to examine the trees. Like all American trees of that time, they were of enormous size, for practically none of them was ever cut down. The Indians could fell few, if any, trees with their stone axes, and even burning them down was difficult. A tree might continue growing for several hundred years.

For some days Cartier and his men had been catching distant, occasional glimpses of wild people, dressed in furs, painted tan, and wearing feathers in their hair. Now, from Prince Edward Island, they saw Indians close at hand, crossing the river in canoes. A little later, a warrior ran along shore, beckoning them to bring their longboats in to land; but when they rowed in, toward him, the Indian, losing his courage, vanished into the forest. Cartier left a knife and a woolen girdle, tied to a branch, to show that the white strangers were friendly.

Two fleets of forty or fifty canoes now appeared. Indians at the paddles made signs of friendship and called out greetings. Cartier wrote down what he thought their greeting sounded like: *Napou tou daman asurtat.* Four hundred years later, after white scholars had studied Indian languages, they discovered that Cartier's Indians had belonged to the Micmac tribe. Micmac words still sound like those Cartier had noted.

Afraid to let so many Indians come too close, Cartier finally frightened them away with cannon. He did not have to shoot directly at them. The explosion was enough.

Next day, nine canoes came back. When the Indians held up furs to show that they wished to trade, Cartier sent two men ashore with knives and hatchets. Never having seen iron tools, the Indians were very eager for them. They gladly sold Cartier's men all the furs they had, even the ones they were wearing, and had to go home to their camps completely naked.

On the Gaspé Peninsula Cartier met about three hundred different Indians, whom he considered a sorry-looking lot. Bits of vocabulary, which he set down again, show that these were Hurons. They possessed nothing of any value except their canoes and fishing nets. They turned out to be "wonderful thieves," stealing anything they could get their hands on, and even snatching things with their toes.

A few days later, Cartier completed this first voyage of exploration, missing the entrance to the St. Lawrence River entirely, because he had sailed up the wrong side of Anticosti Island. He turned back to France, taking with him two young Indians whom he had practically kidnapped.

Eight months later, in May, 1535, Cartier returned, eager for further North American adventurers. He brought with him as interpreters the two kidnapped Indians, who had been learning French during their eight months in France. This time his vessels followed the northern coast of the Gulf of St. Lawrence, a course which brought them straight into the mouth of the great river. From the St. Lawrence, during the next two centuries, other Frenchmen would push southward from the St. Lawrence Valley to the Susquehanna, the Ohio, the Mississippi, the Gulf of Mexico, and westward through the Great Lakes, almost to the Rockies. But it was Cartier who led the way.

Listening eagerly to all his two French-speaking Indians could tell him about the country, Cartier and his men crept up the river, sometimes in their ships, sometimes rowing their longboats close in to shore. Twice they made complete circles, so as to see both banks. It was slow going, for Cartier was desperately afraid of rocks and shoals. The uncharted river was even more dangerous than the Gulf.

In "the great river of Hochelaga"—the name by which the St. Lawrence was known for some time—they found animal life as abundant as it had been in the Gulf. Whales were everywhere. There seemed to be more of them than they had seen on the first voyage. Far up the river, there were still walruses, which they described as "fish in appearance like horses."

The fertile land, the abundant grape vines, the magnificent trees of many kinds, the great numbers of the birds entranced Cartier. "This region is as fine as it is possible to see," he wrote in his notes.

Just below the Indian village of Stadacona, which was later to become Quebec, they met their first large group of Indians, who fled until Cartier's two Indians called them back. Then they welcomed their white visitors with dancing and with gifts of eels, fish, corn, and melons. Other Indians swarmed around, as the news spread. Next day the Huron chief, Donnaconna, came paddling out to the ships, with twelve canoes.

Cartier's two Indians explained to the chief that they had been well treated by the "French chief," in other words, the king of France. Then Donnaconna and his Hurons were given their first taste of French wine and wheaten bread.

Though outwardly friendly enough, Donnaconna had his own suspicions. He refused to allow these mysterious strangers to go on up the river to the village of Hochelaga, later renamed Montreal. To persuade Cartier to go away, he offered some Indian children as presents. When that failed, his Indians made a silly attempt to scare their visitors. Three of them, dressed as devils and making a great noise, came down the river in a canoe. This was answered by an uproar from other Indians, hiding in the woods along the bank.

But Cartier did not scare. With one ship and two longboats, he caught the turn of the powerful tide and started upstream, admiring the country and making notes of everything as he went. Near Hochelaga, he landed and went ahead on foot.

Outside the village, which was enclosed in a log palisade, he passed through cultivated fields, "covered with the corn of the country." This was just ordinary corn, still sometimes called Indian corn. All Americans know it well enough today; but, to these newcomers from Europe, it was new and strange. Cartier noted that the grains were about the size of a pea and that the Indians lived on it, "as we do on wheat."

The village itself was circular. Its log palisade was built in three tiers, like a pyramid. The top tier was built crosswise, the middle one perpendicular, and the lowest one had its logs placed lengthwise. The whole was well joined and lashed together. There was only one gate, which could be tightly barred. Over the gate and at many places about the enclosure were galleries, with ladders leading to them, and in each gallery were piles of stones and rocks, for the warriors to throw on any invading enemy who came near the walls.

There were about fifty houses, each about fifty paces long, and twelve or fifteen in width, built entirely of wood. They were roofed with large pieces of bark, "as broad as a table," cunningly lashed together. Inside each house were many rooms, so that many families could live under a single roof. The Indians were the real inventors of apartment houses. In the middle of the house was a large space without a floor, used as a fireplace. Above the chambers were lofts for storing corn.

Near the village towered a mountain which, in honor of their king, the Frenchmen named Mount Royal, in other words, Mont Réal. Before leaving, Cartier climbed it, to look from its heights far ahead into land he knew he would never be able to explore. He saw mountain ranges, with fine valleys between them, the Laurentian Hills in Canada, the Green Mountains in Vermont, the Adirondacks in New York. He looked longingly ahead, up the St. Lawrence. "As far as eye can reach," he wrote, wistfully, "one sees that river, large, wide and broad."

Here, stretched before him, was the land he had come so far to see. All around him stood red hunters and canoemen, who knew its every inch. It was tragic for Cartier that he could not talk with these Indians, who could have told him all about the distant land where he longed to go—but the interpreters had not come with him.

He did the best he could with sign language. A little way up the river beyond Hochelaga was as far as Cartier was able to explore. Indians indicated to him that there were three more rapids ahead, and that beyond them, one could "navigate along that river for more than three moons." The Great Lakes, about which the Indians were really trying to tell him, were not rivers, but Cartier went home to France with the idea that there was a great waterway leading west, far into a strange land. So much, at least, was true. It was an idea that helped to stimulate other French explorers who were still to come.

It was now autumn, and Cartier turned downstream, regretfully. At Hochelaga on his way back he saw, with horror, five scalps which the Hurons were proudly displaying, "stretched on hoops like parchment."

Near Stadacona, the Frenchmen built a fort in which to spend the winter. Cartier continued his observation of Indian customs. He noted with interest the way the Hurons used tobacco. He had never seen such a habit. He wrote, "at frequent intervals they crumble this plant into powder, which they place in one of the openings of the hollow instrument"—it was a kind of cross between a pipe and a cigarette holder—"and laying a live coal on top, they suck at the other end to such an extent, that they fill their bodies so full of smoke, that it streams out of their mouths and nostrils as from a chimney. They say it keeps them warm and in good health, and never go about without these things. We made a trial of this smoke. When it is in one's mouth, one would think one had taken powdered pepper, it is so hot."

This was probably the white man's first experiment with tobacco, some fifty years before Sir Walter Raleigh began the fashion of smoking at Queen Elizabeth's Court.

Almost as astonishing as tobacco smoking to the French newcomers was the extraordinary indifference of the Indians to North American winter cold. Almost stark naked, they walked through ice and snow in apparent comfort.

In December, the "pestilence" broke out among the Stadacona Indians. This was really scurvy, a disease caused by lack of vitamins. Cartier thought the disease was contagious, especially after some of his Frenchmen became ill. The real reason of the pestilence was that both Indians and whites were living on a restricted winter diet.

Since no one knew what to do, the disease spread till twenty-five sailors were dead and most of the rest seemed to be dying. Then one day Cartier met one of his interpreters, whom he had last seen a few days before, dreadfully ill. Now, the man was in perfect health. This French-speaking Indian explained that he had been saved by drinking a brew made from the leaves of a tree. That, he said, was the only way to cure this sickness. Cartier asked where he could find these miraculous leaves.

The Indian sent two squaws to help the Frenchman gather some. When they came back with branches, the Indians showed him how to grind the bark and leaves for boiling. The sick men at first refused to drink the queer-looking stuff. But when one or two recovered their health and strength at once after trying it, the others likewise drank and were likewise cured.

Within eight days, the French had entirely used up a large tree which, Cartier wrote, "produced such a result that had all the doctors of Louvain and Montpelier been there, with all the drugs of Alexandria, they could not have done so much in a year as this tree did in eight days." The sailors had received the vitamins they needed from some kind of evergreen, which the Hurons called "Annedda." It is supposed to have been hemlock or pine.

With his crew still weak, Cartier became alarmed at the arrival of numerous strange Indians at Stadacona. He decided to start for home, taking Donnaconna with him, so that the French Court could hear from the chief himself the stories he had been telling Cartier about gold, rubies, and other riches. Squaws came aboard with native provisions for him, because the Indians did not think much of white man's food. Carrying the Huron chief as well as the two interpreters, the ships sailed down the river, toward the ocean and home.

Though he never knew it, the explorer barely missed two English vessels, which visited Bird Rock just after the French ships got home. The English, too, got poultry and bear meat on the Rocks; but the expedition under a captain named Hore, accomplished nothing else and barely got home alive.

Cartier came for the third time to the St. Lawrence in 1541, but this voyage added little to what he had already learned of the country. In the meantime, Chief Donnaconna and the other Indians Cartier had taken to France had died. Briefly, Cartier examined the country once more, and then turned back to France.

Cartier had seen the craggy, wooded St. Lawrence with its wild, beautiful scenery he so much admired, for the last time. He was well into his fifties, an advanced age in those days when people did not live as long as they do now.

He settled down in France, an ancient mariner home from the sea, remembering the fascinating sights he had beheld in the New World. His head was full of memories.

In 1557, sixty-three years before the Pilgrims came to New England, Cartier died. How often of an evening he must have strolled down to the harbor of St. Malo, to look west to the setting sun and recall that wild and lovely land where dwelt the red men far across the sea.

But in all his dreams, Cartier could never have dreamed of the things that were to happen in the next four hundred years: That white people would be living in beautiful large cities where the red men's villages had been; that they would be speaking his own language, as well as English; that the wild, free life of the wilderness as well as the Indians, would all be pushed aside, crowded out, to make room for hordes of white people, coming from across the sea in a never-ending stream.

CHAPTER 8

Champlain Goes Farther

1603–1635

F OR nearly sixty years after Cartier's last visit, French exploration lagged. Breton sailors continued to fish for cod, along the Canadian coast. Sometimes their little fishing smacks sailed part way up the St. Lawrence; but, as fishermen, they were not interested in pushing farther inland, where the going was hard. Their business was fish, and salt water fish at that. They caught plenty of them without adventuring upon any fresh-water, inland voyages.

It was a long time before another Frenchman ventured deep into the island-studded waterways and lovely forest country that Cartier had only begun to open up. Cartier seems to have felt, after his fight with scurvy, that this was a land where white men could live only after heroic struggles. His experiences did not attract any one else.

The next great French explorer of North America, the first to enter what is today the United States, did not come till the next century. This was Samuel de Champlain.

He was well trained for the adventurous career that lay ahead of him, for he was both soldier and sailor. He had served in the army of

Henry of Navarre, later King Henry IV of France. He had also sailed in the Spanish service to the West Indies, Mexico, and Panama. Always, Champlain had been interested in strange lands and distant places.

It was natural he should have such interests, for he had grown up in a busy seaport, where all the talk was about voyages and far-off places. He was born in the town of Brouage, France, ten years after Cartier died. The coast of France has changed since then. Today, after four hundred years have passed, the sea has withdrawn. Though the town of Brouage is still there, it is now ten miles inland. Along the wharves and docks of Brouage, while it was still a seaport, Champlain grew up, the son of a naval officer, eagerly listening to seamen's tales of the brave new world that they had seen.

His voyage to the Spanish possessions in America was an extraordinary bit of luck, since the jealous Spaniards usually wanted no foreigners aboard their ships, or in their colonies. No one today knows just how Champlain managed it.

Using his luck to the full, he seized the opportunity to bring back to France a written report of what he saw, illustrated with elaborate drawings. Henry IV, exceedingly pleased to have such information for use in French exploration, rewarded Champlain by granting him a title of nobility, a pension, and the royal favor. The king also arranged for him to sail on a voyage to Canada in 1603, under command of the Sieur de Pontgravé.

Champlain needed little persuasion, for his first sight of the Pacific, at Panama, had fired him with ambition to find the western route to China. It was the same old urge that had spurred Columbus, more than a hundred years before. By this time, everybody knew that the strange continent Columbus had found could not be Asia. Sailors and geographers began to understand at last that there was another and a bigger ocean, west of North America. But they still believed that, somewhere or other, there must be a waterway through the new continent. Along this waterway, they thought, ships could sail straight to Asia. Champlain had at one time hoped the St. Lawrence River was part of it.

No one yet knew how wide a continent North America really was.

No one, French, Spanish, or English, even guessed that the barrier of the Rockies and the vast prairie lands lay between the eastern shore they knew and the Pacific coast that a few Spaniards had seen.

As a friend of the king, Champlain might have lived the soft and easy life of a court favorite. He might have enjoyed government appointments at good pay, with luxury and comfort. Instead, he chose the danger and hardship of wilderness adventure.

Under Pontgravé, Champlain began his career with exploration in about the same area as Cartier. Then, in command of a ship of his own, in 1604, 1605, and 1606, he explored the New England coast, from Maine southward to Woods Hole, Massachusetts. Next he plunged inland, where no white man had ever yet traveled, to explore the Great Lakes and upper New York State. Because winter in the north woods was harsh and dangerous, Champlain did most of his exploring from early springtime, through the summer, returning to France when the American forests were coldest and most desolate.

On his first voyage, under Pontgravé, in 1603, Champlain went straight up the St. Lawrence to Tadoussac. He took with him two Indians he had found in France. How these Indians got to France in the first place, one can only guess. They had probably been taken there by a fishing vessel, or some explorer, now forgotten. Certainly they were not the Indians Cartier had brought back with Donnaconna. They had died years before.

Whoever they were, these mysterious redskins were very useful. They helped Champlain make friends. They also made a great impression among the other Indians, with their descriptions of castles, palaces, and houses in France. Through them, Champlain was able to make the Canadian Indians understand that their white visitors would help them against the Iroquois. Eagerly accepting the offer, the Indians made a great feast for their new allies.

Describing the feast, Champlain says they cooked moose meat in eight or ten kettles, each over its own fire. The Indian braves sat in a row along each side of the log house. When the meat was cooked, each man had his own bark dish, filled with moose. Champlain thought their way of eating was rather dirty. They ate with their fingers and, when their hands became too greasy, wiped them on their own hair or the hair of their dogs. Champlain, remember, was used to the formal manners of the royal court of France, the most polite in Europe.

Champlain's men moved on up the St. Lawrence River to the Lachine Rapids, just above Montreal, where they left their large heavy boats and tried to go on in a skiff. After a few hundred yards they got stuck on a rock. Enviously they watched the ease with which the Indians managed their light canoes, moving delicately around the dangerous rocks that are always near the surface in the churning white water of rapids. It was Champlain's first lesson in wilderness water travel. He realized now he would have to have canoes like those the savages used, not the heavy craft of the white man.

He asked the Indians to map out for him—perhaps only with gestures—the country which lay ahead. They told him of more rapids and open river, until you came to a lake. This was what we call Lake Ontario. Between this lake and another (Lake Erie) was a "somewhat high falls." This was Niagara Falls!

Champlain began to wonder if he had not found, at last, the long-sought passage to the Pacific. But on this voyage he did not attempt to follow the route the Indians described. Champlain soon learned he could not hurry in Indian country. It took time to make friends with Indians, to talk with them, and to visit their villages.

On his next few voyages, Champlain examined the New England coast. Because of this, it was not until June 18, 1609—six years after his first visit to Canada—that he was able to start for the Great Lakes and the country of the Iroquois, which had about the same boundaries as our present New York State.

On the way, he met a band of two or three hundred Indians coming to join him. They belonged to the tribes of the Hurons, Algonquins, and Montagnais. Rashly, Champlain promised to help them against their powerful enemies, the Five Nations of the Iroquois. He could not foresee that he was making permanent enemies for France. A hundred and fifty years later, at the time of the American Revolution, the Iroquois were still hostile to the French, who were then American allies.

When Champlain came to the mouth of the Richelieu River, he

turned south, exploring the river which carried him to the beautiful lake which now bears his name. So long as he was in the St. Lawrence, he was traversing country the French already knew, but as he turned into the broad, deep, and beautiful mouth of the Richelieu, he was striking off into territory no white man had ever seen. Other white men were closer than he thought, however, for at that very time Henry Hudson's *Half Moon* was sailing down the Atlantic coast, on its way to New York.

The wider part of the Richelieu River was easy going, but at the first rapids Champlain found himself handicapped again by his heavy white man's boats. They were too clumsy to be dragged up through the rapids, too big to carry among the thick-set trees on shore.

Canoeing upstream in an inland waterway, it is often impossible to push a loaded canoe against the powerful current. Then the only thing to do is to go ashore, unload, carry everything around the rapids, reload the canoe, and paddle on. Around such obstructions as rapids, there are usually trails, which show that other people have passed the same way. Indians had been using most of these trails for hundreds of years before the white man came. The first white men, being French, called them "portages," or carrying places. The French word for "carry" is "porter." From the French, the word "portage" has passed over into common American usage.

Finding that his men were losing heart, trying to struggle against the current with their heavy boats, Champlain left behind all but two volunteers and set off with Indians in light birchbark canoes. A bark canoe can float on a few inches of water, and one man can carry it over a portage.

A few miles above the rapids, Champlain, with his two white volunteers and party of Indians, reached country in which Iroquois war parties might be expected. When they made bark shelters for the night, his Indians built a barricade of logs around them. Three canoes, with nine men, paddled on ahead for several miles, to see if any enemy Indians were lurking about. They returned to report all clear.

Champlain was shocked to see the Indians go to sleep without posting a guard. When he protested, the warriors replied they had worked hard enough all day. Anyway, their medicine men, having consulted the spirits in his medicine lodge that evening, had said there would be no trouble. Champlain was uneasy about relying upon a message from the spirits. But all was well. There was no attack that night.

Next day they were off again, winding among many pretty low islands, covered with lovely woods and meadows. Game was abundant, providing plenty of good food. Animals were almost tame. The Richelieu River was a war road. In such a place, warriors hunted as little as possible, and the game was left undisturbed.

The next day Champlain entered the lake that was to be named for him—the first white man to see it. As the canoes slipped silently down the lake, the leader gazed about him, enraptured by its beauty. Woods came down to its shores. He saw his first chestnut trees. The huge grapevines were the most beautiful he had ever beheld. He was astonished at fish five feet long. From the west shore, he looked across the lake to the east and saw the Green Mountains, whose outcroppings of white rock looked like snow to him. To the south, he saw other high mountains—the Adirondacks. The country of the Iroquois, in which he was now trespassing, was certainly most beautiful.

As they paddled along, Champlain's Indians described to him another lake, from which a trail led to the Hudson. At the very moment when the Indians were telling him about that mighty stream, Henry Hudson in the ship *Half Moon* was either approaching it or already sailing up its course.

As they were now getting close to the enemy, Champlain's warriors began to travel only at night, halting at dawn and camping in the thickest woods. When Champlain had a dream in which he saw Iroquois drowning in a lake, his Indians were delighted. It was a good omen.

The next evening, as they were paddling silently toward Ticonderoga, the encounter came. Down the lake something seemed to move. It was hard to tell whether those dark spots were snags or swimming animals or clumps of sedge. Champlain's Indians "froze" still—and watched. Soon there was no doubt. An Iroquois war party, probably Mohawks in that region, was paddling up the lake, approaching with equal caution.

The two warrior bands saw each other almost at the same moment.

Since neither one wanted to fight by night, each turned in to shore. The Iroquois hastily built log barricades, while Champlain's Indians lashed their canoes together with poles, so that boats would not be separated if the men had to fight from them when morning came.

Then two canoes paddled over toward the enemy to inquire, formally, if they wanted to fight. The light was bad, replied the Mohawks. Why not start at dawn? Then, instead of sleeping, both bands spent the night in dancing, singing, and shouting taunts at each other. Champlain was speechless with astonishment. But, to the Indian mind, a battle ought to be preceded with a special ritual.

Carefully concealing their white friends in three canoes, Champlain's Indians approached the Iroquois camp next morning. As they reached the shore, the white men slipped out behind the warriors. Champlain managed to get his two men, with their firearms, under cover. The Mohawks still had no idea that their enemies had white men with them.

As the two war parties came toward each other, Champlain showed himself at last, advancing in his gleaming steel armor till he was only thirty paces from the enemy. Champlain looked at them, as they came on, with a soldier's admiration—"strong and robust to look at, coming slowly toward us with a dignity and assurance that pleased me very much." The Mohawks must have been amazed to see a white man, clad in shining metal, approaching them fearlessly. So far as they could see, the stranger had no weapon at all. The arquebus in his hand looked like a mere stick.

There was a moment's pause, while the two groups looked each other over. Then, as the bows were drawn, Champlain let drive at one of the three Iroquois chiefs, easily distinguished by their plumes. Having loaded with four balls, he got three hits, which astonished the Iroquois, who wore wooden armor that was supposed to be proof against all weapons. As Champlain was reloading, his men opened fire from the woods, and in a moment the last Iroquois chief was killed. Throwing away their arms, the Iroquois scuttled for the forest, with Champlain banging away behind them, while his delighted Indians gave chase with knife and tomahawk, until they had killed several more and had captured about a dozen alive.

That night, Champlain saw what happened when hostile Indians caught you. His own Indians began the torture of the first of their victims by burning and scalping him and tearing out his nails and sinews. In horror, Champlain suggested killing him to stop the wretched man's agony. Puzzled by their white friend's scruples, the Indians nevertheless allowed him to finish the miserable business with a single shot—which he succeeded in doing without the prisoner's knowing what was happening.

On the way back, Champlain marveled at the stoicism of the other prisoners, who answered his questions about the Iroquois country cheerfully enough and walked along singing, though they had no hope of being better treated than the one who had already been tortured. It was the traditional behavior of a captive brave. An Indian warrior was taught to be ashamed to fear pain or death.

Champlain's effort to end the horrors of the stake is one of the few cases in which a French officer tried to interfere with Indian torture.

Soon after this adventure, Champlain collected the remainder of his men and sailed home. He left one white youth behind. He was to live with the Indians in the interior of Canada, where no white man had yet penetrated, and to learn their language. In exchange, Champlain took back an Indian boy to spend the winter in France. When he returned, he would thus have two interpreters.

By the beginning of March, 1611, Champlain was back in Canada and was soon talking with the young boy he had sent to winter with the Indians. The lad, wrote Champlain, "explained to me all that he had seen in the winter, and what he had learned from them." But alas! Not one word of all this precious information did Champlain trouble to write down. Not even the name of this youth is known, though he was the first white to penetrate so far into the lake country. The wonderful tale he had to tell of life in unchanged, primitive America was thus lost forever.

Champlain had now won the confidence of his red friends so completely that they offered to show him their country and anything he might want to see there. Back to France he hurried, to get a force of men large enough for the proposed journey.

When he returned, in 1613, his party started up the St. Lawrence

River, often struggling desperately against rapids and whirlpools. The widening of the river, now called Lake St. Louis, pleased him. It was "filled with beautiful large islands consisting of meadows only, where it is pleasant to hunt, deer and game being abundant. There is also plenty of fish. The country surrounding it is full of big forests."

He lost two Indians by drowning and was nearly drowned himself, trying to drag a canoe through rapids. He fell, was caught between two rocks by the force of the current, and could not get the line loose from his wrist. Just as it seemed that his hand would be torn off, the plunging canoe floated into a backwater, and the strain ceased.

It was a hard journey. "We passed some small rapids by rowing, which cannot be done without sweating," he reported. "It takes great skill to shoot these rapids and avoid the whirlpools and breakers which are in them, and the savages do this with a dexterity that cannot be surpassed, looking for side passages and the easiest places, which they recognize at a glance."

Champlain observed one of the most beautiful of American wild flowers—bloodroot. He commented, however, not on the beauty of its blossom, but on its root "which makes a crimson dye, with which the savages paint their faces."

Farther on, the party came to country so wild, with going so difficult, that they had to discard everything, even their reserves of food. They kept only arms and fishing tackle, so that they could get food as they went along. Champlain himself carried three arquebuses—in this way he could get in several shots without reloading. They passed through a region of burnt-over pine lands—the most depressing of landscapes—and were tortured by millions of mosquitoes.

At Muskrat Lake, a local chief was surprised that they had been able to pass the rapids and bad portages at all. If an Indian considered it bad going, Champlain and his men had, indeed, negotiated some difficult canoe traveling. Here, in 1867, was found a bronze astrolabe—an ancient navigator's instrument, now superseded by the sextant. It was probably dropped by Champlain himself, on this very journey. At least, it is hard to think of anyone else who ever had occasion to carry an astrolabe to Muskrat Lake.

Again the summer's end, and the expedition headed home to France.

Returning to Canada in 1615, Champlain went farther inland through the Great Lakes than any Frenchman had ever traveled before. At the Rapids of St. Louis—just beyond Montreal—he found his red friends again begging for his help against their Iroquois enemies. This time Champlain's party, augmented by their Indian friends, traveled along the Ottawa River, regarding that landscape with disgust. Champlain found it unattractive country, with small trees and a great many rocks. Indians did not like it either.

However, it seemed to the explorer that God had wanted to give that desolate region "something in its season to serve for the refreshment of man," and, in this case, God's gift was the blueberry. Champlain thought they were "very good to eat," and noted that the Indians dried them for winter use, as his own people dried prunes in France.

At the point where the Ottawa River turns sharply in a northerly direction, Champlain's expedition turned westward to follow a smaller water route and so came to Lake Nipissing. Spending only two days with the Indians there, the party went on to Georgian Bay, on Lake Huron. On this lake, the French met, for the first time, Indians carrying buffalo-hide shields. Though Champlain does not mention having seen the buffalo herds himself, he was near enough the Great Plains to be meeting Indians from the buffalo country.

Looking out over Lake Huron and questioning his Indians about it, Champlain named it "The Fresh Sea." The Great Lakes, which are the largest bodies of fresh water in the world, naturally seemed like seas to him. He noted the length of Lake Huron at 750 miles instead of 250—probably because he gathered from the Indians the idea that Lakes Huron and Superior were one.

The Frenchmen and their Huron friends soon came to a Huron village near La Fontaine, Ontario, which had triple palisades thirty-five feet high. At the principal Huron village, near modern Orillia, there were two hundred of the long, bark cabins used both by the Hurons and the Iroquois.

The country had greatly changed. Corn, squash, vines, sunflowers, plums, raspberries, strawberries, and nuts grew everywhere. Champlain thought the whole area "very beautiful and attractive." In many places, the trees looked as if they had been artificially planted, "for pleasure."

From the southern end of Georgian Bay, Champlain's party swung back southeasterly, crossing lakes Couchiching and Simcoe, and so came to Lake Ontario.

Hunting as they went, Champlain and his Huron war party worked along the north shore of Lake Ontario, crossing at its eastern end, which is the source of the St. Lawrence River. As they were now approaching the western edges of Iroquois territory, they hid their canoes and started cautiously forward on foot into western New York State. Champlain thought this was most agreeable and beautiful country. Chestnut trees grew in great number, and the nuts were still in their burrs. The French thought they were very good. The American chestnut was—before the blight destroyed all our chestnut trees—much sweeter than the European chestnut.

On October 9, 1615, after they had crossed into New York State, Champlain's Hurons captured three Iroquois men, four squaws, three boys and a girl—all out fishing. He was horrified when a Huron warrior seized one of the women and cut off her finger. Champlain protested, but the Hurons said it was no more than the Iroquois would have done to them! It was just a hint of the tortures that lay ahead. Willing, however, to humor his white friend's queer ideas of humanity, the Huron chief forbade any further torture of captive women; but nothing Champlain could say prevented the Hurons from torturing Iroquois warriors who were their prisoners.

Next day, they reached an Iroquois fort near the town of Fenner, in modern Madison County, N. Y. Old soldier that he was, Champlain found, to his disgust, that nothing would make his Hurons fight as an organized body. He knew enough of their language by this time to shout orders as the fight began. Later, he remarked that he had almost burst his head with shouting. It was no use. Though they had implored him to help them fight their enemies, the excited redskins could not follow out any plan of attack. They fought as they pleased, without co-operation, command, or discipline, every man for himself.

In the end the Hurons withdrew without capturing the village. Like most Indians, they had no taste for siege warfare. Champlain, shot in the knee with an arrow, had to be carried in a kind of basket to the place where they had left their canoes. The only good thing he could say for his Hurons that day was that they made their retreat with great security, putting all their wounded and old people in the center, surrounded on all sides by armed warriors and keeping this arrangement until they had reached a safe place.

They found their canoes undisturbed. Far enough away from their enemies now, the Hurons paused to hunt. They built a stockade in the form of a triangle, with its base open and a narrow opening at the top leading into a small enclosed yard. A line of beaters, moving through the woods at dawn, frightened the deer into the wide open end of the triangular stockade. Once the deer were inside, they could easily be forced through the small opening into the enclosed yard, where they were killed.

Champlain now encountered one of the strange Huron superstitions. These Indians refused to roast any of the meat or let any fat or bones fall into the fire. What you did with the bones of both game and fish was very important, they told him. Future success in hunting depended upon it. Bones had to be treated respectfully, for the souls of some dead animals returned to see what was done with them. The Indians believed they would never be able to kill any more game, if the dogs were allowed to gnaw on these bones. Beaver wanted theirs thrown back into the river or burned, and "the trap which has caught them is glad of this." Fish, on the other hand, objected to having their bones burned, but did not mind being caught and eaten.

This time, Champlain had to settle down for several wintry weeks in Indian country. In December, he set out for the country of the Petun, or Tobacco Nation, who lived southwest of the Hurons, probably in Dufferin and Gray counties in modern Ontario. Not used to traveling on snowshoes and dragging his heavy duffel on a birch toboggan, he suffered severely as he moved through the icy forests with their tangles of fallen timber. Even so, he was pleased with the country, whose hills and woods and little fields made a pretty, snow-covered landscape.

The Petun Indians were friendly, as were the Ottawas, whom he next visited. Champlain thought these Indians kept their households cleaner than any others he had seen. They worked industriously making mats of various patterns, which they used for rugs. Thus he passed on, from tribe to tribe, on the best of terms with all the redskins, except the Iroquois, and so came to Montreal and to the end of his career in exploration.

He became a prisoner of war when English raiders seized Montreal, but was eventually released and allowed to return to France. At last, when the war was over and Canada had been restored to France, he came back as governor in 1633. He died in Montreal, on Christmas Day, 1635. It was an even hundred years since Cartier had begun the exploration that Champlain had carried so much farther. Champlain had been the first white man to visit New York State, the home of the Iroquois Five Nations. He was the first to see how Indians lived there at a time when the primitive land and the wild animals were at their very best. Champlain has been called the father of French settlement in Canada. Within a few years, settlers began to cluster along the St. Lawrence and commenced fur trade in the land he had opened up for them.

CHAPTER 9

"We Were Caesars"

Lake Country: One

I N SPITE of Champlain's adventurous journeys along its borders, the beautiful Iroquois country in New York State was still largely unknown to white men. Champlain had passed down part of its eastern edge, when he cruised south on the lake that now bears his name. He had fought his battle with the Mohawks on the New York side; but, after the battle, New York was hostile country, which he dared explore no further. On his western trip, Champlain had penetrated a little way into the state from Lake Ontario; but, again, there had been fighting and he was stopped. Champlain's subordinate, Étienne Brulé, actually made a trip from western New York to the Susquehanna, in a vain effort to get the help of warriors there. But Brulé's report was never written down. Nobody knows what he saw— probably not very much, as he traveled in danger of his life at every moment.

The next advance in French exploration was made by the daring Canadian, Pierre Esprit Radisson. He was the first to visit and explore central New York. After that, with the aid of his brother-in-law, he pushed west far into the Great Lakes area and probably even beyond the Mississippi.

Toward the end of his life, Radisson wrote down his story—wrote it in some of the wildest syntax that has ever masqueraded as English. Radisson had little education to begin with. Probably he did not write even his native French very well. While he was with the Iroquois in New York, he was getting his information in the Mohawk language, or the related Iroquois dialects. Later, he had to do the best he could with the languages of the western Indians.

If he had been content to tell his story in French, even though he had a wild jumble of Indian names and half-understood Indian languages in his head, all might still have been well. But, being in the English service in his later years, when he set down his story, he insisted on writing in English—another language that he did not understand very well.

Most of the time, the reader can see what Radisson means. At other times, the reader can guess, with some hope of correctness. In other passages, there is no hope at all of figuring out the meaning.

As a boy, the future explorer lived in the Canadian frontier settlement of Three Rivers. One day, in the spring of 1652, Radisson, then sixteen, went out from the fortified settlement, to hunt ducks with two French companions. After going about a mile, the three boys met a man herding cattle, who warned them to keep away from the hills. He had seen Indians in that direction, he said, suddenly rise up from the earth. These were Iroquois, who hated the French and constantly lurked about the settlements in the hope of catching just such incautious wanderers from the fort as these three boys.

After killing a few ducks, the others started home, but Radisson recklessly went on alone. When he, too, finally turned homeward, he was carrying three geese, ten ducks, a crane, and some teal. But he was not to reach home with his day's good catch.

Alarmed by a sudden sound, he reprimed one pistol, searched the woods without seeing anything suspicious, and went ahead. He was just about to fire at some more ducks, when he stumbled on the dead bodies of his companions. Both were naked. One had bullet and tomahawk wounds, the other several stabs and marks of the tomahawk. In his sudden fear and excitement, Radisson began to bleed at the nose. The experience was enough to drive anybody's blood pressure upward.

Making for the river, he was startled to see twenty or thirty heads bob up out of the long grass. Hastily, he dropped a bullet down the barrel of his fowling piece, on top of the light birdshot with which it was already loaded. But it was too late. He suddenly found himself surrounded by Iroquois, rising from the grass, the rushes by the river, and the bushes. He got in one shot from his fowling piece and one from his pistol before he was seized by the happy Indians, who were now laughing at him and howling like wolves.

Once they had dragged their prisoner back into the woods, the raiders showed him the scalps of his two friends, who had so gaily started off with him that morning. One of the worst experiences of Indians' captives was to recognize the scalps of their friends and relatives, gleefully exhibited by the savages who had killed them.

Radisson saved his life by his boldness, which made a good impression on the Iroquois from the start. This good impression he confirmed a few days later when, prisoner though he was, he gave a terrific pummeling to a young warrior who insulted him. Above all things, Indians admired bravery. They liked white prisoners who stood up to them. When they saw Radisson's courage, they began to be friendly. Though at first they stripped him of his clothes and, for a time, tied him up, they soon gave back his clothing and began to feed him. The meat they offered him was tainted and foul smelling, but it was all they had and exactly what they were eating themselves.

When, however, the warriors saw that he could hardly choke it down, they cooked up a new mess. That was not much better, but Radisson managed to eat a little.

As they grew more friendly, his captors began to comb and grease his hair. They even painted his face red, making him more like themselves. When they began to pass through regions filled with game—moose, deer, beaver, waterfowl—they gave him a shot at a stag and let him have a knife. Occasionally, as they plodded along the trail an Iroquois would say to him, "Chagon!" which means, "Cheer up!" Gradually they began to give him more and more liberty.

They moved down the Richelieu River to Ticonderoga, Champlain's route, but an old Indian warpath long before that. Thence they went down Lake George and portaged over to the Hudson. As they approached the Mohawk villages, twenty squaws came out to meet them, bringing dried fish and corn for the warriors. Then, as was the Indian custom, they loaded the squaws with their baggage.

In spite of their friendliness, as they entered the village, the Iroquois prepared to make Radisson run the gantlet. This did not indicate hostility. It was as a warrior once explained, "a sort of how do do," besides being a convenient and entertaining (to Indians) way of seeing which prisoners were sturdy enough to be worth adopting. Indians always set great store upon physical courage and endurance. They admired men and boys who could endure severe pain and still keep smiling. Running the gantlet was a kind of character test.

The Indians, armed with long sticks, stood in two lines facing each other. The prisoner had to start at one end and run between the lines, while the yelling crowd tried to hit him. No matter how fast one tried to move or to dodge from side to side, it was impossible to run the gantlet without getting a beating.

After Radisson had been stripped for his ordeal, an old squaw came up to him and threw a covering around him. This meant that her family was adopting him, and that he did not have to run the gantlet after all. No longer a prisoner, he was taken to his new "mother's" cabin, clothed, fed roasted corn, and had his hair combed and greased again. Radisson had had the great good luck to be adopted by a famous and extremely good-natured warrior, whose whole family soon became devoted to their new white kinsman. From then on, the white boy lived the life of a carefree young warrior, playing most of the day with his young companions. Two daughters of the lodge combed and greased his hair every morning and carried his pack for him, when he started on a hunting trip. They named him after their dead brother, Orimha. The Mohawk name meant "stone." By pure chance it corresponded with Radisson's Christian name, Pierre, which also means "stone."

As he was now a member of the tribe, he was allowed to go about freely, even to leave camp to hunt. Ranging the woods with three Mohawks, Radisson found game so plentiful in eastern New York that, in a single day, they killed three bear, one stag, and a beaver. The French boy watched in admiration the skill of his red companions. Once, when they had to cross a wide stream, the Indians built a canoe in two hours.

All would have gone well with Radisson, had they not met an Algonquin prisoner, also from the vicinity of Three Rivers. Like Radisson, this prisoner, too, was trusted to go hunting alone. Speaking only in Algonquin, a language which the Mohawk-Iroquois could not understand, this man persuaded Radisson to help him tomahawk the three hunters, as they lay sleeping that night. Radisson hated to do it. These Iroquois companions had done him no harm. But he hardened his heart by remembering that their people and his were mortal enemies and that the Iroquois had burned and murdered many of his French relatives. During the night, he and the Algonquin killed the three sleeping hunters and escaped to the St. Lawrence. But near the river they were seen by some lurking Iroquois, who gave chase. The fugitives threw the three scalps into the water, but the incriminating evidence floated long enough to be seen by the pursuing warriors.

They killed the Algonquin at once and dragged Radisson back to the village he had left. He tried to tell the story that the dead Algonquin was responsible for the murders and he himself had been the Algonquin's prisoner. No one believed him, and he was put to torture. This time he did not escape the gantlet and was severely beaten. As if this were not enough, other Iroquois struck him with fire brands and rods of thorn.

His Iroquois parents, much distressed, finally rescued him and took him to their bark cabin. His Indian father scolded him but, at the same time, brought him food.

Again he was taken out for torture. For two horrible days the Mohawks played with him, like a cat with a mouse. They tore out four of his fingernails, and made him sing while they did it. When he became speechless with pain, they made him drink something to bring him to again. Tied to a post, he was forced to watch while they burned other prisoners alive. In the end, the pleas of his devoted Mohawk mother, father, and brother saved him once more. After he had been nursed back to health, he managed to escape to the Dutch settlement at Albany. From there he was sent to France.

Most men would, by this time, have had enough of life beyond the frontier; but Radisson was of the breed to whom the wilderness calls. He was one of those with curious minds who had to go and see. Most of the early explorers had other motives for undertaking their travels into unknown lands, but in men like Radisson and Champlain the dominant motive was the lure of the great woods, the wild, free life, the strange new peoples, the satisfaction of going where no white man had been, the hunt, still lakes at dawn, new plants, strange animals, the silent overarching trees, the spice of danger.

For these unreasonable causes that could never be understood by townsmen safe in houses, many explorers and frontiersmen—British, American, French, and Spanish—risked their lives and salted North America with their bones for three centuries, until at last they had seen it all, there was no more left to explore, and the whole continent was white man's country. Of these was Radisson.

Reaching France early in 1654, he stayed only a few months, and then was off for Canada again. Another man might have been content in the French settlements that were now along the St. Lawrence. Not Radisson. It is reasonably certain that he and his brother-in-law soon started west, and that they went as far as unknown Lake Superior. They probably reached Lake Winnipeg, to the northwest of Lake Superior and halfway across the continent. They knew of a lake called "Ouinipeg," which meant "stinking water," and of the Indians called "Puants" (Stinkards) because they lived on its shores.

Two years later, the pair returned in triumph, accompanied by a fleet of fifty canoes, filled with Indians from the various tribes around the Great Lakes. These strange Indians wanted Frenchmen to go back with them to spend the winter in their country. They wanted missionaries, too.

But the only missionaries were Jesuit priests, then on the point of starting for the wilderness near Syracuse, N. Y. The hostile Iroquois were showing signs of friendship at last. They had already asked for Frenchmen to live among them, and a party had already gone ahead of the missionaries to build a fort. The Lake Indians would have to wait.

Radisson joined the party that was going into the Iroquois country with the missionary priests. Why, with all North America to explore, he chose the part most dangerous to himself, there is no explaining. Twice in the past he had had to escape from the Iroquois. This time he hoped for safety, so long as he was among the Onondagas, and not the Mohawks, but he had to run the risk of being spotted by a visiting Mohawk.

With an Iroquois escort, the party approached the American boundary by way of that widening of the St. Lawrence known as Lake St. Francis, southwest of Montreal and just above New York State. Radisson thought this was most delightful and beautiful country. They shot moose and waterfowl as they went along.

But, however beautiful the country, the journey itself was marked by a horrifying and bloody incident. After making peace with the French and with their Huron allies, the Iroquois had persuaded a group of trusting Hurons to return with them and settle in Iroquois country. On the way something happened to change the minds of the Iroquois. Perhaps some incident of the trail irritated them. At any rate, they murdered the Huron men, sparing only the squaws and one old man. After this, they placidly put a kettle on the fire for supper and called a council. The priest was summoned to hear what Radisson called "their wild reasons." Some Iroquois had been drowned by accident, they said, and it was necessary to revenge that upon the Hurons! The white men were horrified, but there was nothing they could do but sit down with the murderers for supper, hope for the best and keep their arms handy.

In spite of this, Radisson was enchanted by the game they saw as they passed into New York State. Deer were so plentiful, they took time to have some sport. Once, driving a deer into the water they paddled up beside it and hung a bell on its neck. Then they laughed to see the deer try to get back with its companions who, alarmed by the sound, ran away from it.

Once, at twilight, a large number of bears walked past their camp. They were making a horrid noise, breaking small trees, and pushing rocks down by the water side. They paid no attention to shots, a peculiarity which in itself frightened the men, so that no one wanted to leave camp in the gathering dusk to follow the animals and see what they were doing. It was remarkable to see so many bears at one time, but it may have been an incident of their mating season. In our day, bears behave in a quite different way.

As Radisson's party moved toward Lake Ontario, the St. Lawrence became more and more beautiful, so wide and open they could move for stretches of fifty and sixty miles with no portaging. An Indian shot an eagle for its feathers. Ospreys, herons, and king-fishers flew about, snatching fish from the water. The canoemen could kill salmon with nothing but clubs, and they hauled a sturgeon up from six fathoms. The water was so clear, that even at such a depth, the bottom could be seen easily, with fishes moving above it.

A Mohawk war party, returning home, passed them and recognized Radisson. They showed no resentment at his escape, but asked when he was coming to see his friends. He said, "Soon," and sent gifts to his Mohawk family.

Radisson was one of a party who ventured too far out on Lake Ontario during a calm and then was caught in a sudden storm. The others got to shore, but Radisson had to ride it out. A bag of corn hung over the bow of his canoe, steadying it. The gunwales of the boat were only three inches above the white-capped waves.

Passing along the Oswego River and Lake Onondaga on their way to the village of Onondaga (near modern Syracuse, N.Y.), Radisson found central New York a charming and fruitful country. In some places it stretched for several miles at a time, "smooth like a boord," he wrote. There were fields of Indian corn, several fields of a vegetable Radisson called "french tournaps," many chestnuts, oaks loaded with acorns, with "thousand such like fruit in abundance." Among these fruits were "stoneless cherries," which the Indians called atoka— Radisson meant cranberries. Passenger pigeons were everywhere. You could take fifteen or sixteen hundred in the net at once.

Onondaga resembled the Iroquois village that Champlain had seen and the Huron village at Hochelaga that Cartier had described. It had the usual palisade, the fortified gate, and, inside, the "long houses" of bark—primitive apartment houses each of which sheltered many families.

The travelers saw salt springs yielding a brine so strong that they were surrounded with a crust of crystals. The passenger pigeons clustered around these, perhaps because they craved the salt. Other springs held magnesium and sulphur in their waters. A still more wonderful spring had "water" that burst into flame when touched with a firebrand. It was, of course, a place where petroleum leaked out of the earth and floated on the surface of the spring. Indians used the fluid to oil their hair and bodies. It became known to white men as "Seneca oil," and was supposed to be a valuable medicine. The Indians burned it in torches in the bows of their canoes, when they speared fish by night.

But things began to go wrong, in this earthly paradise. As the Onondagas showed increasing signs of unfriendliness, the handful of Frenchmen and their friends decided to leave while there was still time to get away alive. They made a feast for the Indians—one of the "eat all" feasts, at which it was a point of honor for the guests to swallow every morsel of food set before them, no matter how much of it there was. While the Onondagas were sleeping off their tremendous gorge, the travelers slipped silently down the river. A hog tied to a bell made noise enough inside the fort to convince the Indians that the Frenchmen were still there.

After his adventure with the Mohawks, this narrow escape would have quenched any ordinary man's desire for wilderness life and exploration. But this time, as before, Radisson had hardly reached safety in the Canadian settlements when he was eager to be off again. He wanted to "travel and see countries," as he liked to phrase it. His brother-in-law, who had already been on Lake Huron, was just starting off to discover other great lakes he "had heard the wild men speak of." From his description, these were not the Great Lakes as we know them, but probably the innumerable lakes to the north and west of Superior, and perhaps Hudson Bay, into which these lakes drain, for Radisson names a "Bay of the North."

Two priests were going along to convert natives in that remote country. Accompanying them were a mixed group of about one hundred and forty—some white, some Indian—hoping to make a profit from furs.

Up the now-familiar St. Lawrence they started. Radisson began to have doubts about the new white people in his party. Canoemen ought to keep quiet and they ought to keep together. These fellows let their canoes straggle out for six or eight miles along the river. Those who felt like it landed casually to kill game. Radisson knew that Iroquois war parties were pretty sure to be lurking somewhere along the St. Lawrence and Ottawa Rivers, on the lookout for just such incautious persons. He soon understood that his new traveling companions were amateurs who knew nothing about the big woods or the dangers of wilderness rivers. Some of them could not even swim.

When Radisson and his brother-in-law tried to warn the greenhorns of the risks they ran, the foolish fellows simply laughed. The Iroquois, they were certain, would never dare attack them. In their ignorance, they "knew it all." Radisson reflected bitterly they knew nothing of the hardships that lay ahead, had never endured Indian torture, had never seen the cruelty of a war party.

An Iroquois attack soon followed, of course. Thirteen men were killed before the enemy could be beaten off. That was enough for the greenhorns, once so self-confident. They hurried back to safety in the settlements. But, for the third time, the lure of the big woods proved stronger in Radisson than fear of any possible danger. He and his brother-in-law went on with their Indian friends, determined to "finish that voyage or die by the way."

They very nearly did die. Food ran short. Berries were not yet ripe. Game was scarce. They had to fall back on the last resort of the northern wilderness traveler, tripe-de-roches. This is a moss or lichen, which grows thickly on rocks along the lakes, and looks enough like bits of tripe to justify its name—tripe of the rocks. Boiled, it turns into a sticky mess, something like glue, with a bad taste and worse smell, but with the sole advantage that it slips down quickly and prevents starvation.

The going grew harder as the two *voyageurs*—the French name for wilderness canoe travelers, a word still in common use in the northern lakelands—paddled on up the Ottawa River. Soil began to disappear, until at last they could see only rock and sand. To Radisson, it seemed a miracle that large trees could grow from mere cracks in the rocks, apparently with no earth at all. In this rough country, moccasins and leggings swiftly wore out. There was no way to replace them till the travelers could kill moose or deer, which would provide leather as well as meat. The sixty portages they had to cross were so overgrown that thorns scratched feet, legs and thighs until they were covered with blood.

It was an immense relief when the light canoes shot out over the chill, clear waters of Lake Nipissing. Here, bear and deer were plentiful. They could get meat, make leather, and repair their footgear. The lake was full of fish, which they could see through water clear as crystal. One must see such lakes to understand how pure water can be. They are filled with rain water only. It has fallen through woodland air, which has no dust, upon clean rocks, or on a forest floor where roots hold the soil so firmly in place that there is no muddy water. Thus are produced the "clearwater lakes," which look like rocky basins of distilled water. They are specially clear because they are so cold that micro-organisms cannot grow, to cloud them.

Even today there are a few such lakes, where one can look through twenty feet of water to see pebbles on the bottom and fishes moving as if they swam in nothing, the water itself being almost invisible. When the wind is still and these lakes are smooth, they take the color of the sky, so that the canoes seem to be moving through the air itself. Once this liquid crystal has flowed through the swamps that often lie between the upland lakes, deep in the big woods, and the lower lakes, it has lost its amazing purity. In most of the lower lakes, nearer to settled country, it is just the usual dull lake water—not particularly clear, not very murky. That is the only kind of lake most modern white men ever see.

Where there were so many fish, otters were certain to be plentiful. These beautiful and playful creatures were so swift that they could catch a fish, swimming under water. Their fur, even then, was valuable and easily taken, for the animals had been little hunted. Radisson complained that there were so many they "gathered to hinder our passage." They did, indeed, delay him, for the Indians insisted on pausing to hunt them. They had to shoot them with arrows, not daring to use firearms, since they had seen the footprints of other Indians, who might be hostile.

The travelers found many hindrances. There were places where beavers had felled trees for their dams. Sometimes the beaver ponds thus produced covered large areas. In other places, the ponds had filled with silt and become "trembling ground," where neither man nor canoe could move. There were quicksands ready to swallow up any man or animal that stepped upon them. There were muskegs— swamps peculiar to the north woods, filled with masses of decayed, water-soaked vegetation and silt, dotted here and there with spongy patches of moss or grass, which commenced to sink when a man stepped on them. Indians taught Radisson to go on all fours, when these tufts of grass seemed likely to sink with him. This distributed weight, so that one could creep from tuft to tuft, dragging a canoe through the mud and water.

Just where the two Frenchmen went, after passing Lake Huron, no one knows. Radisson's own geography is vague. There were no maps. Often he himself did not know where he was. Rivers, lakes, mountains, villages that he passed had only Indian names, which cannot always be identified. The names of the tribes he visited are sometimes vague and do not necessarily tell where he was, for the tribes were always moving. He had no way of keeping a diary. He made no record at all, until many years later, and by that time his memory was somewhat confused.

Nevertheless, it is perfectly clear that Radisson and his one white companion penetrated far enough southwest of Lake Huron to find a beautiful river. It was so large, wide, and deep that it reminded Radisson of the St. Lawrence River. This sounds very much as if he had seen the upper Mississippi, though he is not usually credited with being its discoverer.

In the spring of 1660, the two came back down the Great Lakes and the St. Lawrence, bringing a great store of beaver skins. As they approached the French settlements, they encountered an Iroquois war party but fought their way through successfully.

After about a year, in June of 1661, they were off again. These men could never stay in safe and civilized places. The beautiful still country of endless lakes, everywhere dotted with islands, manifold in shape and size and even color, was something such voyageurs could never resist. When the wilderness beckoned, something in the way they were made forced them to respond and paddle away.

The beauty, strangeness, and wonder of the wilderness far out-weighed the hardships of such a life. The times when food was short, when they had to sleep on bare rock, on wet or swampy ground, chop their way over a portage, or crawl like frogs over muskeg, reach-ing from one tuft of moss to another; times when they went for days and nights in the rain, when they paddled with aching muscles over stretches of rough water, all these fell in the background of the mem-ory. The enduring recollections were ever the changing beauty and wonder of the earth and water, the endless entertainment spread before them by the wild creatures of the woods, the fish and water animals, the birds of the air, the strange tribes.

This time, they paddled along the north shore of Lake Huron from Georgian Bay, then portaged round the Sault Sainte Marie into Lake Superior. Farther west in the Superior country, Radisson found a pool where large waterfowl were nesting. He called them "bustards," but they must have been wild geese. When he tried to creep stealthily in among the nests to keep from frightening the birds, he found to his amazement that the birds were trying to frighten him! They had not learned to fear man.

Indians showed him bits of Lake Superior copper lying on the forest floor. They told him he need not weigh himself down with specimens. There was plenty more of it ahead. In one place there was a whole mountain of copper, or so the Indians said.

Radisson exulted in the abundance the new country offered. Every-where he went, he found something new. He thought the wild new lands that he had found fully as fruitful and beautiful as those the Spaniards had found in the South. Radisson wanted France to have a part of the new continent. Rumors of Spanish exploration, passing from tribe to tribe, were now reaching the northern Indians; but Spain had not reached the Great Lake country. Radisson and his com-panion, as the first white men there, could claim it all for France.

They spent a desperately hard winter in the wilderness. Once more the game had vanished. Red men as well as white grew gaunt from hunger. This was somewhere to the western end of Lake Superior. During the winter a Sioux delegation visited them to request a "thunder," that is, a gun. Presents, including three hundred beaver skins, were showered on the Frenchmen by various tribes.

Toward the end of the winter, they went to visit the Sioux in their own country—probably Minnesota. They were surprised by the big buffalo-skin tepees of the Sioux which the squaws could pitch in less than half an hour.

Spring and summer of 1663, they spent with the Cree, north of the Lakes. Slowly then they worked their way back to Montreal, as usual fighting their way through Iroquois war parties along the St. Lawrence.

Safely home at last after all their hardships, they now received a painful shock. They had gone into the woods without a government license. The French governor confiscated the whole stock of furs they had brought back at the risk of their lives. Furious at such treatment, both men left Canada and entered the service of the English king, Charles II.

Later, Radisson returned to Canada for more exploration along the coasts of Hudson Bay, far to the north. For a little while he joined the French again, then went back to the service of the British. He was living in England for some time before his death. In these last years, he wrote down what he could remember of his travels in unknown lands. It is a pity that he did not keep a journal, as he went along. The story, as he told it, is stirring enough; but scores of incidents must have escaped him. He seems to have liked, best of all, the lakelands of the wilderness. Here, he said, he and his brother-in-law felt like Caesars.

CHAPTER 10

Vérendrye and His Sons

Lake Country: Two

IN SPITE of all this exploration by the French and Spanish, no one had yet crossed North America to that distant Western Sea about which explorers had been dreaming since Columbus. Not till fifty or sixty years after Radisson's travels did another French adventurer begin to feel that call of the unknown western sea which recurs, like a persistent refrain, in the stories of early American exploration.

Pierre de Varennes, Sieur de la Vérendrye, is one of the greatest, yet the least known, of the North American explorers. Most Americans now living in the States that he explored hardly know his name, though Canadian children learn in school of his achievements.

Vérendrye was a native Canadian who became an army officer in the French service. As a lieutenant he received four saber cuts and a shot through the body in the "very murdering battle" at Malplaquet, where French, British, Prussians, Dutch, and Austrians were all engaged. In all, he was wounded nine times during his service in Europe. Then, finding he could not live on a French officer's pay, he gave up the army and returned to his own country. He married and settled down, for the only quiet years of his arduous life, on his property near Three Rivers. Here were born the four sons who were to share his adventures.

As his family grew, Vérendrye began to look around for some way to make a better living than his trading post at Three Rivers afforded. He secured command of the extreme outposts on Lake Nipigon, immediately north of Lake Superior. Though French canoemen had already pushed two or three hundred miles beyond this to Rainy Lake and Lake of the Woods, the Nipigon posts and Fort Beau, the post among the Sioux, were the westernmost establishments thus far made permanent. Except for the canoe routes along what are now the "border lakes," between the United States and Canada, there was no real knowledge of what lay beyond; but always there were the rumors of a route to the Western Sea. Vérendrye questioned the Indians who came from the lake-and-forest country westward, to trade with him.

Yes, the red men told him, there was a great river flowing west. It flowed at last into the sea. What the simple children of the forest said was true, but it was extraordinarily misleading. None of these early explorers westward seem to have had any idea of western distances. The great river flowing west was something like 3,000 miles away.

In 1728, Vérendrye, bubbling with enthusiasm for western discovery, visited Michilimackinac—between Lakes Huron and Michigan—where he met Father Gonner, one of the two missionaries then working among the Sioux. The priest had seen enough of that formidable tribe to feel sure there was little hope of passing through their territory to the Western Sea. He was therefore ready to share Vérendrye's enthusiasm for a route along the border lakes. Vérendrye had already prepared an outline of his plans, which Father Gonner offered to take to Quebec and urge upon the governor.

Vérendrye himself returned to Lake Nipigon, where he continued to question Indians. Tacchigis, a Cree chief, told the eager Frenchman that he had traveled as far as "the lake of the great river of the west." Other Indians had told Vérendrye the same thing. Eagerly he continued to question the Cree. Did Tacchigis know of any more great rivers? Yes. From a height of land sloping to the southwest—which must have been somewhere in Minnesota—he had seen four great rivers. He was pretty clearly referring to the Red River of the North, the Saskatchewan, Big Elk River (a stream of no great importance, which flows into the Rainy River), and the headwaters of the Mississippi—though these cannot all be seen from any one point.

Another Indian, a slave held by the Cree, told Vérendrye that the western lands were full of tribes who "raise quantities of grain, fruits abound, game is in great plenty and is only hunted with bows and arrows; that the people there do not know what a canoe is; as there is no wood in all that vast extent of country for fuel they dry the dung of animals." He added that he had seen "the mountain the stone of which shines night and day, and that from that point you begin to notice a rise and fall of tide." This was probably a reference to the Rockies and perhaps even to the estuary of the Columbia River. The Rockies were often called "The Shining Mountains" because the sun glittered on their snowy summits. Early explorers thought these were shining rocks. Nobody climbed the mountains to find out.

Vérendrye chose an Indian as guide for his journey. Ochagah, the guide, drew a map of the region from Kaministiquia (near modern Fort William, Ontario) on Lake Superior, all the way to Lake Winnipeg. He probably drew on birch bark which has long since crumbled; but luckily a copy of his map still exists. It shows the "Shining Mountains," but it shows them standing close to Lake Winnipeg, and Lake Winnipeg is north of North Dakota. The Indian's map also shows Lake Winnipeg west of Lake of the Woods, whereas it is actually almost north of it. Other Cree drew other maps for Vérendrye, and told him wonderful stories of western lands rich in minerals, teeming with game, so filled with beaver that Indians living there threw their beaver-skin robes away every spring because they could not sell them. This suggested an enticing idea: there must be a fortune in the fur trade in such a country.

Vérendrye returned to Quebec in 1730 to present all this information to the French authorities. Reminding the French governor that "the English have every interest in getting ahead of us, and if we allow them time they will not lose the chance of doing it," he got permission to build a new fort in the West, as a base for further exploration toward the Western Sea. But the government would not give him a sou to help pay expenses. Instead, they told him he could have a monopoly of the fur trade in the new regions. This was of no use to any one else, since no white man had reached the lands where Vérendrye was going. He was thus forced to run into debt to equip his expedition. Worse yet, it was not long before the officials who had authorized his engaging in fur trade were attacking him for doing so. Yet the fur trade was his only possible chance to finance the government's own expedition.

By the end of August, 1730, Vérendrye reached Grand Portage, on the northwestern shore of Lake Superior, the "big portage" which led into the border lakes. Here there was trouble with his men, who became frightened when they saw what toil and danger lay ahead of them. They became mutinous. Vérendrye compromised by sending three men—including one of his sons and his nephew, Sieur de la Jemeraye (who was also his trusted lieutenant)—on to Rainy Lake, while he himself wintered with the others at Kaministiquia.

In the spring he pushed on, joined the other three, and the party paddled down the short Rainy River, into Lake of the Woods, where they built Fort St. Charles. This was a strong wilderness fort with a double palisade, fifteen feet high and a hundred feet square, with four bastions, houses, a chapel, and a powder magazine.

The size and abundance of fish in these lakes would have been a modern fisherman's fantastic dream. One of Vérendrye's fishing parties caught 4,000 big white fish, besides trout, sturgeon, and other species. In winter, the Indians built huts over holes in the ice. Looking from darkness into the water, they could see down forty or fifty feet and spear fish with very long poles.

In this lake country one could not go hungry. The shallow waterways were full of wild rice, which attracted waterfowl. Even so, Vérendrye burned the trees and underbrush over a tract large enough for a wheat field, and planted it.

So far, the Indians' maps of his route had been correct, he reflected happily. The rest of their stories must be equally true. He talked to twenty Cree, taking them separately, one by one. Their stories all agreed.

For the next few years, Vérendrye remained at his fort. He kept down tribal wars, as well as he could. He had trouble making friends with the Assiniboins, who were alarmed because they had heard that the French had come to eat them. He listened to marvelous stories of a strange tribe, the "Sioux who went underground"—really the Mandans or Arikaras, both of whom lived in earth-covered lodges. While Vérendrye was hearing about these distant tribes, they had been hearing about him. Presently he received an invitation from a Mandan chief to pay his tribe a visit.

By the spring of 1735, Vérendrye hoped to start out for the Mandan country. In the meantime, however, there were other things to be done: He sent two men to make friends with the Indians on Lake Winnipeg, and then one of his associates took ten men there to build a fort. A Cree chief adopted one of Vérendrye's sons, who went off with his new "father" and other Cree to Lake Winnipeg.

Vérendrye himself went back to Montreal with a cargo of pelts. Now the government, which from the first had refused to pay him or even provide supplies, even objected to his effort to pay for the expedition by fur trading, though they had told him he could do so. The problem was settled by allowing him to farm out his fur-trading posts to merchants, while he himself devoted his time entirely to exploration—still at his own risk and his own expense.

He returned to the wilderness and to tragedy. His nephew, La Jemeraye, was killed west of Lake of the Woods. Soon afterwards, hostile Sioux—catching his son, one of the priests, and about twenty of their men on an island in Lake of the Woods—killed them all. As the bodies were found lying in a circle, Vérendrye concluded they had been treacherously attacked while in council. The Sioux had cut off the heads and wrapped them in the beaver skins for which the Frenchmen had been so eager. It was a typical bit of grim Indian humor, such as they exhibited years later when they killed early American frontiersmen. Their bodies were sometimes found with their mouths filled with earth—because they always wanted land!

Questioning the Indians on Lake Winnipeg, he heard more stories about the Mandans. He now learned that the river on which they lived—the Missouri—did not run west but turned south, entering the ocean at a place where, his Indian friends told him, "there are white men, towns, forts, and cannon, and where prayer is said, there being priests in the country." Vérendrye felt sure the Indians must be talking about the Spanish setlements on the Pacific coast. Actually, they were trying to give him a description of the Missouri, from the Dakotas to St. Louis, and of the Mississippi to the Spanish settlements along the Gulf coast. Even now, almost 250 years after Columbus, no one had guessed at the enormous length and breadth of North America.

Two years later, in October, 1737, Vérendrye was back again in the French settlements. By this time, he was in his early fifties. Instead of showing an appreciation of all he had done, the governor at Quebec blamed him for leaving his post. He warned the explorer that if he came down to the settlements again, he would not be allowed to return to the wilderness. Reports had been sent to France and complaints came back from the bewigged, perfumed, and lace-ruffled French Court. They were surprised that the explorer had made so little progress towards the discovery of the Western Sea. They referred to the massacre of the twenty-one men beheaded by the Sioux as "most annoying." They could not imagine the difficulties of wilderness life and travel, nor the time required for calming the red man's natural suspicions of white intruders and making friends with them.

With fresh supplies, again bought at his own expense, Vérendrye returned to the new fort on Lake Winnipeg. He reached there in September, 1738, and made preparations to go himself to the Mandan country, at last. The local Cree made all kinds of objections to his going: They told him the Assiniboin River was low and he would ruin his canoes. The Assiniboin Indians, through whose country he would have to pass, were themselves a queer lot. They didn't even know how to kill beaver, like proper Cree! Their only clothing was buffalo skin—outlandish garments which the French would not want anyway. They were "people without intelligence" who would not get along with the white men. It all sounded as if the Cree were afraid of losing some of their fur trade with Vérendrye.

Paying no heed to all this talk, Vérendrye went up the Assiniboin River, the first white explorer to see it. He went as far as he could go. There had been no rain all summer. It was now the end of September and the river was very low, with many shallows and yet a strong current. Trees lined the banks, but he noticed that there were no conifers. This meant that there would be no gum or resin to repair his bark canoes if holes were punctured in them; no way to calk new ones if his canoes were wrecked in rapids. Beyond the river lay a boundless stretch of prairie in which were buffalo and deer.

Leaving his men to bring the baggage and canoes, Vérendrye himself struck off overland for six days into more new country, meeting increasing numbers of friendly Assiniboins, until he came to the portage at the modern Canadian town of Portage La Prairie. Here he built a new fort, farther west than any Frenchman had yet traveled, and here the rest of his men joined him.

In mid-October, with about twenty men, Vérendrye struck off southward on foot, following an ancient Indian trail. This was a trail used by the Mandans who were agricultural Indians and traded their surplus corn as far north as Rupert's Land. The party were much delayed by an Indian guide, who, like most Indians, traveled only when he felt like it. They were further delayed by Assiniboins who insisted Vérendrye must pay them a visit. One chief came to meet them accompanied by his whole village, of forty lodges, and they were delayed for a day or more because the chief wanted to see more of the Frenchmen. Vérendrye had scarcely gotten his party started again when his guide insisted on a detour of sixty or seventy miles to visit another Assiniboin village. Here, each warrior put his hand on Vérendrye's head, taking him for "father," and then on the other Frenchmen's heads, taking them for "brothers," meantime crying as hard as he could. Because of this Assiniboin custom to weep on such occasions, the French called them "Weepers."

When Vérendrye got started again, the whole Assiniboin village set off for the Mandan villages with him.

After crossing a mountain (probably Pembina Mountain) their

route was over rolling prairie, a perpetual succession of small hills and valleys. The prairies were almost wholly grass, with only occasional clumps of trees. So infrequent were these little groves that the Assiniboins loaded their dogs with firewood. In emergencies they made fires of dry buffalo chips, known to the French as "bois de vâche," or wood of the cow.

Old soldier that he was, Vérendrye observed with respect the march discipline of the Assiniboins—scouts ahead, detachments on each side in contact with a strong rear guard, and women, children, dogs, and old people in the middle. Women and dogs carried all the baggage, for these Indians had no horses. The moment a buffalo herd was sighted, the scouts yelled the news and all the most active warriors rushed forward to join the hunt. Killing buffaloes on foot was risky business, but no one was hurt and there was soon plenty of meat.

Assiniboin runners were sent on ahead to tell the Mandan chief what to expect. He was glad to see the Frenchmen, who brought valuable trading goods; but he was appalled at the thought of feeding all the Assiniboins who had come along. Indian hospitality always included feeding visitors, but such a horde was a problem.

Before long, the Mandan chief thought up a sly trick for getting rid of the hungry Assiniboins. He was, he said, glad to see them, because he was expecting to be attacked by the Sioux very soon and needed help. The chief knew quite well that the Assiniboins lived in constant terror of the Sioux.

His scheme worked fairly well. Most of the Assiniboin women and children with a guard of men, were left some distance from the Mandan village. For a little while, it looked as if the Mandans would still have to feed six hundred hungry warriors. But they finally scared them off with a new report of a Sioux attack, while the Mandan chief slyly motioned to Vérendrye to stay where he was.

From the Mandan village, Vérendrye examined the new country as far as he could. The Missouri River was muddy, not very good for drinking. Broad, filled with shoals, studded with snags and tangled masses of trees, its swift current swept past the explorer, flowing from the unknown to the unknown—to the Western Sea, he hoped. It was hard to get any idea from the Indians, who were too eager to talk.

One Indian interrupted another when they tried to speak. Often, too, they failed to understand his questions. Vérendrye thought the river might turn west or southwest before it reached the sea, where, the Mandans told him, there were men like himself, dressed in cloth instead of skins.

Interpretation was a problem. Vérendrye spoke French to his son, who spoke Cree to their interpreter, who spoke Assiniboin to any Mandan who happened to understand it. Though it was a roundabout way, it was better than the signs he had to use sometimes. But there was plenty of room for misunderstanding in any conversation which had to pass through so many intermediaries.

The exact spot Vérendrye reached is not easy to determine. He had crossed from modern Ontario into North Dakota and was certainly not very far from Bismarck. He was probably at the Mandan village near Armistead, North Dakota, some fifty or sixty miles above Bismarck. In Vérendrye's time, before the great smallpox epidemic—a result of too many white traders' visits—which nearly destroyed the tribe, Mandan villages were scattered for many miles along the river.

He was much surprised by the earthen Mandan lodges, large and warm and comfortable. The Mandans were agricultural Indians, who stayed more or less near home instead of wandering, as most other tribes loved to do. They built permanent villages, laid out in streets and squares. The streets were kept clean. The lodges were made of a framework of logs as large as our telegraph poles, over which earth was piled several feet thick. This mass was then shaped into a rounded dome.

The biggest Mandan lodges, specially built for ceremonies, could accommodate two hundred Indians. The lodge of an ordinary warrior had room for forty or fifty people, as well as for their animals. A fire in the center of the lodge kept it warm, even through Dakota winters. The Mandans never thought of chimneys, but let the smoke escape through a hole in the center of the roof. Under the lowering walls of the dome, planks divided the large dwelling into small quarters for family groups. It was like dividing off sections under a big tent. Personal belongings were stowed away in leather bags. Beds, raised about two feet from the ground, were made of stretched fresh buffalo hides, which tightened as they dried.

The whole settlement was surrounded by a palisade to keep out invaders and prowling animals. Around this, in turn, was a big ditch, fifteen or more feet wide, and about as deep. One could enter only on wooden steps, which could be removed in time of danger. Vérendrye thought the arrangement very clever, very advanced, for savages. Indeed, it makes us think of the medieval castles of Europe, surrounded by their moats, with drawbridges across them.

Secure and warm in their villages, the Mandans lived well and, with an abundance of buffalo meat and corn, they rarely suffered from the famines that often menaced the northern Indians. They varied their buffalo meat and corn diet with antelope, deer, beechnuts, squash and pumpkins. Vérendrye said his hosts set more than twenty dishes before him every day.

Mandan corn did not produce the big ears we know today. Their ears were no larger than a man's thumb, but they had a great many of them. They stored dried corn for winter use in pits dug six and seven feet deep into the ground.

The explorers ate Mandan dinners frequently. They could not talk with the Indians, but it was friendly to eat with them. They ate from earthen pots, with spoons and ladles of buffalo horn. Later, when white pioneers used similar utensils, someone invented an oath that was to become common on the American frontier: "by the great horn spoon."

The Mandans cooked better than most Indians. They could boil meat properly by hanging their earthen kettles directly over the fire, instead of clumsily dropping hot stones into a kettle made of bark as the Assiniboins did. Most tribes did not learn to boil meat without hot stones until the white man came with his iron and brass kettles. No wonder the Indians wanted every metal utensil that white men could give them.

Today one may see a Mandan Indian lodge at Fort Lincoln, Mandan, North Dakota—across the river from Bismarck—a memorial to the first human inhabitants of that part of the world.

For the time being, Vérendrye had gone as far into the unknown interior of the mysterious continent as he could. December, 1738, was already partly gone. He could return overland on foot to the Assiniboin River, but beyond that he would have to travel by canoe. To do that, he must get back before the spring floods began.

Leaving two men behind to learn the Mandan language, he started over the wind-swept, bitterly cold prairie. Beyond the wide Missouri, he and his sons could see small hills and undulating prairie, unexplored, endless, tantalizing—calling, calling to those adventurous, eager spirits. Somewhere beyond lay the Shining Mountains and the Western Sea. Into that land the Vérendryes wanted to go.

By February they were back on the Assiniboin, Vérendrye himself sick and exhausted. "Never in my life," he wrote, "did I endure so much misery, pain and fatigue as in that journey." The two men he had left among the Mandans rejoined him in September. They told him that they had talked with strange Indians who had come overland from territory where there were Spaniards—white men who "prayed to the great Master of Life in books." One of these strange Indians had worn a cross and often said the names of Jesus and Mary. Clearly these Indians had come from the southwest, and had heard the teachings of Spanish missionaries.

The distant white men, the Indians said, had firearms, horses, and cattle. Their women were "very white and handsome, wearing their hair in a coil and earrings of brilliant stones, with bracelets and collars of very light yellow; and by imitating the movements he showed them that they played the harpsichord and the bass viol."

This was interesting news. Vérendrye sent one of his sons to the Mandans to inquire further, but he left no story of that journey. The young man returned, however, with cotton cloth and porcelain beads, which had been made by Spaniards. He also brought two horses—the first that white men had seen on the western plains. It was now over two hundred years since De Soto and Coronado had brought horses to the West and it was once thought that some of these had escaped and bred. It is more probable, however, that most of the wild horses of the plains and the horses, which the Indians soon learned to ride, really came from Mexico. Some of them may have been strays. A good many of them were stolen by the Indians.

At last, in April 1742, Vérendrye's two sons pushed on beyond the
Missouri River. Indians of the border lakes were at war with the
Sioux, and Vérendrye himself was busy trying to keep them quiet.
Being now familiar with the route, they made a quick journey to the
Mandan villages. Here they waited for two months, expecting the
arrival of a visiting tribe, whom they describe as "Gens des Chevaux,"
or "Horse Indians," probably Cheyennes.

When these Indians failed to arrive, two Mandans offered to serve
as guides, and the Vérendrye brothers set off. The fascinating journey
took them over primitive, unspoiled Dakota plains, and perhaps into
Nebraska, Montana, and Wyoming. There were still no maps, of
course. The Vérendryes could indicate their route only by compass
bearings, without even rough guesses at the length of each day's march.
They failed to learn the real names of the tribes they met, identifying
them only by French names which mean nothing today. They kept
no daily log but waited until their return to write down what they
could remember. It is impossible to tell now just where they went.

For twenty days they moved on foot, west-southwest, and in all this
distance they saw no Indians—only many wild beasts. This gives one
an idea of how empty North America was in those days.

They passed the colored Bad Lands along the Little Missouri, for
their journal describes "earths of different colours, as blue, a kind of
crimson, grass-green, shining black, chalkwhite, and ochre."

It was August before they reached the "Mountain of the Horse
Indians," perhaps what is now known as the "Cannonball." As Indians were likely to do when they went too far from home, one Mandan guide began to get nervous, and soon would go no farther.

After months of travel, the Vérendryes had still failed to find Indians. They halted, built a lodge, and lit fires all around them as signals, hoping the "Horse Indians" would turn up. At the end of a
month, the homesick Mandan started back.

In mid-September, to their joy, the Frenchmen saw a smoke. It
was an encampment of Indians they called the "Beaux Hommes"—
who may have been identical with the Crows. Whoever they were,
they were good-natured and cordial. Though the second Mandan
guide now went home too, leaving the white men without a transla-

tor, they learned enough about the language of their new red friends to get along pleasantly with them. After some weeks camping together, both whites and reds set out south-southwest, passing from one now unidentifiable tribe to another. These new Indians were well supplied with horses and even had mules and jackasses. Some Indians they met could speak a little Spanish.

With a war party who may have been Cheyennes, the Vérendryes went on through magnificent prairies until they saw distant mountains, from whose summits they hoped to behold the Western Sea. They came to the very foot of the mountains, which, they now saw, were covered with many kinds of trees and were very high.

At this moment, the Indians with them became suddenly alarmed. They feared that another tribe, whom they called People of the Serpent, might attack their home villages, while they themselves were absent. No one knows who the People of the Serpent were. They can hardly have been the naturally peaceful Shoshones, whom later white men sometimes called Snake Indians.

When the warriors decided to return, there was nothing the Vérendrye brothers could do but return with them, most unhappy not to have been able to cross the mountains. They did not have the faint consolation of knowing that, even if they had crossed them, they would not have seen the Western Sea, which was still a long way off.

They could console themselves with the thought that they had gone farther westward than any other white man, though the Spaniards had already come about as far in the opposite direction. Just where the Vérendryes went will never be known. They must have seen the Black Hills in the southwest corner of South Dakota. Perhaps they had gone as far as Caspar, Wyoming. They can hardly have reached the Rockies or they would have commented on their snow-capped summits.

Fortunately, one important point in their journey is definitely fixed. They paused at the junction of the Bad River and the Missouri, directly opposite the site where Pierre, South Dakota, stands today. Here, on March 15, 1743, they found a band of Indians, probably

Arikaras, who lived there until the Sioux drove them out fifty years later.

The elder Vérendrye had, years before, left with the Mandans an engraved lead plate, such as other French explorers had buried here and there, claiming the country for France. The sons, too, had carried a lead plate through all their journey. They decided this was the place to leave it. On a hill overlooking the river, they built a pyramid of stones, on which they placed "a tablet of lead with the arms and inscriptions of the king."

There it lay, undisturbed, for 170 years.

One Sunday afternoon in February, 1913, schoolboys in Pierre were taking their girls out for a walk, when one girl noticed a small bit of dull metal sticking up from the ground. She dug around it, loosened it, and picked it up. The others gathered to look at it, and one boy made out the "number" 1743. They were nearly ready to throw it away, when one girl said it might be a tablet of Moses. Maybe it was "worth something." They took it home.

This was the old marker of the Vérendrye explorers. It is now the chief treasure of the South Dakota Historical Society.

Since the explorers feared that the Indians might regard the placing of the tablet as bad medicine, they took care to do it secretly. One of the sons wrote in the journal that the Indians "did not know about the tablet of lead that I had put in the ground."

In the following April, the Frenchmen returned to the Mandan village, passing a group of friendly Sioux without adventure. From the Mandan village they went on to the Assiniboin, after a minor skirmish with another band of Sioux—this time, hostile. They rejoined their father in July, 1743. This was the end of the Vérendrye explorations in the United States, though they still had more ahead of them in Canada.

The adventurous Vérendryes had seen a vast deal of our young country during their years of arduous travels, but they never had a glimpse of their goal—the Western Sea. The land was big and time was fleeting. It would require another half century and a few years more, before white men would cross the mountains and walk on the western shore.

CHAPTER 11

The English Come to Virginia

IT IS astonishing now French and Spanish explorers hovered about the great, empty land of North America in the early years of the sixteenth century—only fifty years after Columbus, or even less. All at the same time, De Soto was exploring the South, Coronado the Southwest, Alarcón the Gulf of California, and other Spaniards the California coast. At nearly the same time Cartier was sailing up the St. Lawrence waterway. The Spanish would have been there, too, if Cabeza de Vaca had been willing to lead the expedition. But Cabeza de Vaca had had enough of North America. He went off to South America instead.

The English were slower than their competitors, in spite of the early start in North American exploration that the Cabots gave them. An English ship commanded by an Italian captain, John Cabot, had cruised along the Canadian coast in 1497, only five years after Columbus's voyage. His son, Sebastian Cabot, in command of another English ship, had nosed along the Atlantic coast the next year, passing New York harbor without seeing it. But not until 1584 did the

English again try to establish settlements in America. Then two bold and brilliant subjects of Queen Elizabeth began to meditate schemes for adding new country to their queen's dominions.

When, in 1565, the fierce Spaniard Menéndez butchered the Huguenot colonists in Florida, a handful of the Frenchmen had the luck to get safely away into the forests. When they dared venture back to the Florida coast once more, they had the extraordinary good fortune to be picked up by a passing English vessel.

One of the Frenchmen was Jacques Le Moyne, an artist who had come with the French Huguenots to make pictures of the new world. In London, whither his English rescuers took him, his paintings of strange plants, strange animals, and Indians, who were strangest of all, greatly interested three of Queen Elizabeth's courtiers. These were the half brothers Sir Humphrey Gilbert and Walter Raleigh—already eminent though not yet a knight—and also the gallant soldier-poet, Sir Philip Sidney.

With one exception, Le Moyne's paintings have long since vanished; but they had at once attracted the attention of a Flemish artist, Theodore de Bry, who made engravings of them. These engravings were used to illustrate a queer little book written by the expedition's carpenter, Nicolas Le Challeux, another of the few survivors of the Menéndez massacre. Le Moyne's pictures were extremely vivid, as one can see by the two shown in this book. It is not surprising that they stirred the eager imagination of the Queen's boldest adventurers.

Sir Humphrey Gilbert persuaded his queen to grant him a royal patent for American exploration. But alas, it did him little good, for Sir Humphrey died at sea in 1583. As his ship went down, he shouted cheerfully across the water to another vessel that the way to heaven was "as near by sea as by land." His patent then passed to his half brother, Raleigh.

Two ships sent out by Raleigh reached North Carolina not far from Cape Lookout, in July of 1584. Coasting north, they slipped into Pimlico Sound and made their first landing on one of its southern islands. When they celebrated their arrival with a musketry salute, the noise startled a great flock of white "cranes." The explorers were nearly as startled as the birds, which rose in the air "with such a cry as if an army of men had shouted altogether." The white "cranes" were either egrets, ranging very far north as they still do, sometimes, or else very young blue herons, which have pure white plumage before full growth.

It was the newcomers' first glimpse of the vast flocks of waterfowl that haunted creeks, marshes, and rivers all over North America. The marshy ground was full of woodcock, plover, and snipe, the lakes and streams with wild ducks, wild geese, heron, and strange birds like the great whooping crane, now nearly extinct. The seashores swarmed with birds, as Cartier had found, including the great auk, now wholly gone. The banks and streams were filled with valuable fur-bearing animals, too, like beaver, otter, muskrat, and "minxes" (minks).

Except in one or two favored spots there is nothing like it today. In those days there was nothing to disturb the herons, ducks, and wild geese, which nested freely where they wished; waded and paddled in streams whose banks are now thickly populated, and feasted on frogs, tadpoles, and fish which have long since been driven from waters now polluted by the growth of human population. The Indians killed freely, of course; but no Indian wastes game and the numbers they could kill with bow and arrow made no inroads at all upon the huge flocks that came and went each spring and fall. As the numbers of white people increased, the vast flocks of waterfowl decreased. The white man also enjoyed killing for sport, and the deplorable waste of wild life began.

Enraptured, these first English visitors, accustomed to the neat, well-trimmed English landscape, gazed about them at the wild luxuriance of primitive North America. The height of the trees in the primitive forests especially impressed them. They commented upon "the highest and reddest Cedars of the world" and oaks, "far greater and better" than any in England.

At some seasons, the forest itself was more fragrant than the air which blew seaward from it. The English newcomers counted fourteen different kinds of sweet-smelling trees. One reason for the fragrance of the southern woods was the magnolias, which one observer

called "the fine Tulip-bearing Lawrel-Tree which has the pleasantest
Smell in the World."

Going a little farther along the coast, they made a temporary settlement on Roanoke Island. The hospitable Indians here feasted them
on venison, roast fish, melons, boiled roots, fruits of various kinds, a
tea made of wild ginger and sassafras, and wine made from wild
grapes. This is one of the few cases on record of wine-making among
the Indians. The "wine" may have been nothing but fresh grape
juice, gone a little old.

Since there were no interpreters, conversation had to be wholly by
signs. This led to some bad misunderstandings. One Englishman
tried, by signs, to ask the name of the country.

"Wingandacoa," was the reply.

We would probably have a state of Wingandacoa in the Union today, if Queen Elizabeth had not wanted the new land named Virginia,
in her honor. As a matter of fact, Wingandacoa was not the name of
the country at all. The warrior of whom the question had been asked,
did not have the least idea what the Englishman making signs at
him, meant. But, feeling that he had to say something, this very polite
redskin had politely replied: "What pretty clothes you are wearing!"

When this first expedition returned to England with glowing accounts of what they had seen, Raleigh made preparations to send another ship in 1585, commanded by one of the greatest of the queen's
seamen, Sir Richard Grenville—soon to be famous for his battle to
the death with the Spaniards. This time settlers came, and with them
Thomas Hariot, eminent man of science—sent out to make a reliable
scientific report on the new country and its resources. Grenville himself, after landing the settlers, sailed back to England.

The Indians were not so friendly this time—probably because they
began to realize that these white strangers had come to stay. There
was some fighting and much difficulty in getting the natives to share
food supplies.

The white men did not understand how to live off the country,
rich though it was. Food ran short. Matters were becoming desperate
when Sir Francis Drake sailed in with a fleet of twenty-three ships,
on his way round the world. He gave the hungry settlers food sup-

plies and then offered them a ship of 170 tons burden to take them back to England. Since he had recently captured twenty Spanish ships, he could well afford to spare one. By 1586, the people who had intended to settle in Virginia were safely back in London.

Scarcely had they left America, however, when Grenville sailed up Pimlico Sound, with supplies from England. Bewildered at finding no trace of the people he had left he landed supplies anyhow. With them, he put ashore a small group of new settlers, under the impression that the settlers of the year before must be somewhere about. So far as he knew, they had had no opportunity to leave and there were no signs that they had been attacked.

When, in the following year, 1587, three more ships arrived, this colony, too, had vanished. Weeds growing about the cabins showed that the settlers had been gone some time. More daring adventurers went ashore to stay, but when in 1589 another little fleet put in, these settlers were likewise missing. Grass grew over heavy metal objects that they had abandoned. Various chests had been buried and then dug up again by someone. John White, their returning leader, who had been in the new colony on an earlier trip, found his books, maps, and pictures mouldering on the ground.

The missing colonists were never found, nor has there ever been any genuine trace of them. In 1937, a carved stone, which told briefly of the party's fate, was discovered, but this was soon proved to be a fraud. It was nothing but a forgery, made only a short time ago. Years after these colonists disappeared, Indians told the Jamestown settlers that the white people had lived in native villages until Indian medicine men decided they must be killed. Only four men, two boys, and one "young maid" were saved. The girl was almost certainly Virginia Dare, the first white child born in the country that is now the United States.

In spite of these disasters, the English kept sending settlers to Virginia. Their obstinate efforts to start a colony there, after the first one in 1584, are especially well reported, since their leaders were educated men, who had to send news back to London, where Raleigh took a strong scientific interest in what they found. Hence the story is far better recorded than most early ventures. Not only are there written reports. Pictures of Indians, plants, fish, even insects were made on the spot by John White, one of the leaders. White was a competent draughtsman and painter, with a keen interest in botany and zoology.

The first permanent white settlement in the United States was made at Jamestown, Virginia, in 1607. Before long the English newcomers were pushing inland, up the James River to the falls at Richmond, and about fifty miles beyond, in other words halfway between Richmond and Charlottesville.

Not far beyond this point, they hoped to find the Pacific Ocean! These early Virginians thought that one branch of the James River came from high hills about ten days' march distant; that once they got over these high hills they would find "that peacefull Indian sea" —the Western Ocean of centuries of dreaming. The only thing wrong with these ideas was the existence of about three thousand miles—America's vast middle land of broad prairies, her biggest river, and the Rocky Mountains.

Though the first Virginians endured hardships, they were delighted with their new country. They loved the mildness of the air, the fertility of the soil, the situation of the rivers, the wonderful big trees, the abundance of game, oysters, fish, and the many, many other new things to see.

In some places rainfall left glistening minerals so thickly along the banks of streams that the very ground seemed gilded. This raised hopes of finding gold and other precious minerals, though the glistening objects were only bits of quartz, mica, or iron pyrites. The Jamestown people sent two ships back to England with "this gilded Dirt," before they found out their mistake.

They were not the only ones to make it. Bartholomew Gosnold, exploring the New England coast, eagerly eyed the glistening minerals he found on an island off Cape Cod. He took loads of this earth back to Europe, only to find it worthless. The early French along the St. Lawrence took home so many shining crystals of no value that in France the phrase "a Canada diamond" came to mean anything worthless.

There was something else that sparkled in America, which they had never seen at home. Fireflies were entirely new to white men. They were familiar with glowworms, crawling insects that give off light, like fireflies. But tiny sparks of light moving here and there through the air were entirely new. "Glowworms here have wings," said one Englishman. There were so many fireflies that the first time he saw them he thought the heavens were on fire.

The Virginia explorers were about the only ones who paid any attention to the insect life about them, though some of the French kept an eye on the possibility of raising silkworms. When the Virginians stumbled upon some trees on whose foliage the fat green larvae of some species of the big American Saturnid moths were feasting, they thought they had found silkworms. They were, in a sense, silkworms, but not the kind that can be easily used to make commercial silk.

Interest in the silkworm was developing in England. The English colonists, delighted to find Virginia mulberries, on whose leaves the silkworm fed, growing wild, imported some eggs. The worms grew until their "master workman" fell sick, at which time rats ate them. That was the end of silkworm raising. Since then there have been many efforts to develop a silkworm industry in the United States, but it has never succeeded.

The same early English writer who commented on the fireflies did, however, pay attention to another insect—quite unintentionally. This was when he spied a fruit which he thought looked like a pineapple, though it was "of an Ash Colour." He took hold of it—only to be stung by an emerging swarm of angry hornets, so severely that his companions could hardly recognize his swollen face.

The English colonists noted the big, yellow tiger swallowtail butterfly, which floats so gracefully about modern flower beds all summer long. They had a quick eye for birds too, and enjoyed the songbirds as well as the game birds. They enjoyed the cardinals, bluebirds, and the gay colors of the parroquets, now probably extinct.

These first English colonists were delighted by the food American plants produced for them. Like many other new arrivals, they found the wild strawberries surprisingly large—four times the size that grew in England. They liked the wild onions that the Indians scorned and were surprised at the size of the sweet potatoes which grew "as big as a Boy's Leg" in the redskins' gardens.

Not all the strange plants and fruits were quite so agreeable. The Virginians' greatest botanical shock was their first experience with persimmons. They tasted them thinking they were plums. It did not take them long to discover that, before the frost touched this fruit, they would "draw a man's mouth awry with much torment." After frost, they tasted "like raisins dipped in honey."

Other Englishmen were seriously ill when they ate the leaves of the Jimson weed, which they gathered to make a "boil'd Salad." Some temporarily lost their sight and others their reason, though they all seem to have recovered. Every now and then modern American doctors have similar cases.

In Virginia, the black bears roamed near the coast, where Indians hunted them. White men and red men alike thought bear meat was about the best there was. The English settlers tried to buy it from the Indians, who kept it for themselves. Bear meat was best in the fall of the year when the animals fattened themselves on acorns, before they went to sleep for the winter.

With the 1607 settlers came Captain John Smith, whose life held adventures enough for three men, for he attracted adventure as a magnet gathers iron filings. He had fought against the Turks in Hungary, had been captured, then sent as a slave to Tartary, where he killed his master and escaped through the Crimea and the countries around the Danube to Poland and finally home to England.

America was to provide him with a whole new series of adventures. He began at once to explore the country adjoining the new Virginia settlements. He explored Chesapeake Bay and the rivers that empty into it—the Susquehanna, York, James, and Potomac, together with the smaller tributaries.

He met with the adventure that has made his name known to every American school child, while he was exploring the Chickahominy, a river that enters the James, a short distance above Jamestown. Here he was set upon by a large party of Indians, who had already killed the two men left to guard his canoes. For a time he defended himself by holding his Indian guide in front of him, like a shield, making a vigorous defense and killing three of his assailants. But, as he retreated, he stepped into a swamp, sank, and was taken prisoner.

The Indians would probably have killed him, then and there, had he not, with great presence of mind, gotten them interested in his pocket compass, with its wavering needle. Eventually they carried him as a prisoner through several Indian villages, to show him off, before taking him to Chief Powhatan.

At first Powhatan seemed friendly. Then—or so Smith understood —the chief demanded that his white prisoner should help him in a raid against the Jamestown settlers. When he refused, according to his own account, he was laid with his head on a big stone and warriors stood ready to beat out his brains with clubs. At this moment, the chief's daughter, Pocahontas, perhaps twelve or thirteen years old, laid her own head above the white man's and so saved his life.

The truth of this story has been doubted, mainly because John Smith did not tell it in the first edition of the book of adventures he later wrote. He put it in only after Pocahontas had aroused interest in London, which she visited as an Englishman's bride. But, after all, a thing is not necessarily untrue because it appears in the second edition of an author's book. Furthermore, it can easily be shown that very much the same thing happened to other white men. There is no real reason for doubting the truth of this story, especially as some of Smith's tales of amazing adventures in Hungary have, in very recent years, been shown to be true, by early Hungarian documents.

Captain Smith left some interesting reports on the abundance of Virginia fish. He claimed to have taken fifty-two sturgeon at one haul and sixty-two at another. This was extra good fishing; but it was not unusual for a net dropped into a Virginia river to take six or eight of the big fish, in four or five hours. One fisherman describes how he took enough sturgeon and other fish at a single haul of the net, to load a ship. Six and nine foot sturgeon were taken and one writer even reports them sixteen feet long! The last story sounds suspicious but there is no doubt these fish were very large. Even today, a six-foot sturgeon is not unknown in Minnesota.

Where there were so many fish, there were bound to be fish hawks. Now the English saw for the first time a familiar drama of America wilderness skies—the big bald eagle forcing the smaller fish hawk to give up its prey. This can still be seen. The fish hawk, or osprey,

INDIANS KILLING ALLIGATORS

Engravings by Theodore De Bry from drawings of Jacques Le Moyne, who was one of the Huguenot colonists in Florida 1562-66. From *The New World* by Stefan Lorant.

FORTIFIED INDIAN VILLAGE

The shore of Roanoke Island, very much the same today as when the first English settlers landed there.

t' Fort nieúw Amsterdam op de Manhatans

Hartgen's View of New Amsterdam, the earliest known picture (c. 1626).

The Cataract of NIAGARA. some make this Water-Fall to be half a League while others reckon it no more than a hundred Fathom.

Panel from a map made in 1711. "A view of the Industry of the Beavers in Canada in making dams to stop the course of a rivulet to form a great lake, about which they build their habitations." Also an early drawing of Niagara Falls.

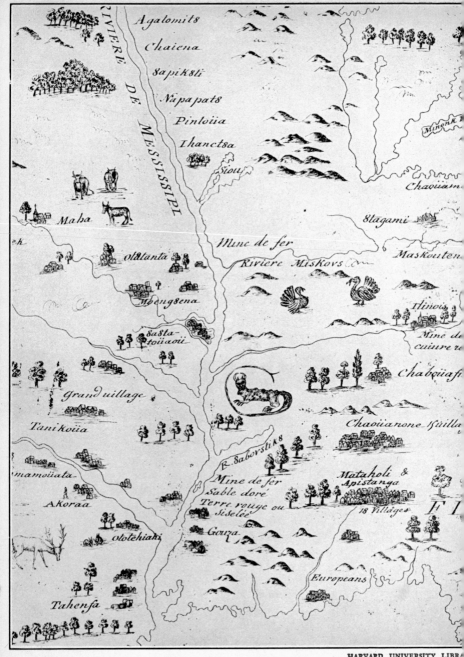

Parkman's copy of an early map of the upper Mississippi, showing the Indian clif
painting of the Piasaw monster.

Minnetaree village of earth-covered lodges on the Knife River, painted by George Catlin in 1848. Photo from the Smithsonian Institution.

Nineteenth-century representation of the Piasaw Rock near Alton, Illinois.

Florida swamp. From *Picturesque* America, 1872.

Canebrake in Alabama, which formerly covered vast areas
in the Southeast and lower Mississippi region. From
Economic Botany of Alabama by Roland M. Harper, 1913.
Courtesy of the author.

Forest scene on the Lehigh River in Pennsylvania. Engraved from a painting by Karl Bodmer (c. 1830).

The site of Washington, D. C. Engraved from an early 18th-century painting.

Canyon of Rapid Creek, in the Black Hills. From Reynolds' *Exploration of Wyoming and the Yellowstone,* 1859-60.

Indians hunting buffalo, a painting by Charles Wimar, 1861.

Two drawings from *Exploration of Wyoming and the Yellowstone,* 1859-60.
Above: Bear Butte in the Black Hills. Below: Citadel Rock on the upper Missouri.

Swamp on the Mississippi, from a painting by Joseph P. Meecker.

Bluffs of the upper Missouri. Painted by Karl Bodmer. From *Travels in the Interior of North America* (1832-34) by Maximilias Wied-Neuwied.

Carolina parroquet and Passenger pigeon, from Mark Catesby's *Natural History of Carolina, Florida and the Bahama Islands*, 1754.

The Great Auk, from the engraving of Audubon's painting.

Sea Otters, photographed by Robert Jones in 1949.

Hypothetical reconstructions of Indian dwellings in Chaco Canyon, Arizona. Painted by Robert Coffin.

Montezuma Castle, Indian Ruin, Prescott National Forest, Arizona. Photo by Edgar L. Perry.

The St. Lawrence River and Montmorency Falls, from Ile d'Orléans. Engraved in 1809.

The engraved lead plate left by the Vérendryes at what is now Pierre, South Dakota, March, 1743. Courtesy of the State Historical Society of South Dakota.

Indian paintings on a cliff at North Hegman Lake, Superior National Forest.

Curtain Falls, on the International Boundary Canoe Route, Superior National Forest, Minnesota.

Here the American landscape remains as it

Virgin red and white pine along the shores of Boulder Bay, Boulder River and Lac la Croix, Superior National Forest, Minnesota.

Primitive Forest of white pine type near Elk Butte, Idaho.

re the pollution of the white man.

Scene in Lolo National Forest, Selway Wilderness area, Idaho

Buffalo Crossing the Yellowstone, painted by Charles Wimar, 1859.

plunges into the water to capture its fish. As it rises with its catch in its talons, the eagle hovers above it, threatening to attack, until the osprey drops its fish—which the eagle instantly seizes.

As time passed, more settlers arrived. Virginia became a safe, prosperous, civilized colony. Slowly, the Indians drew back, retreating westward, ever westward, as the white men took more and more land. A few years before the American Revolution, Virginia had reached to what is now Albemarle County, at the foot of the great Blue Ridge. Men with curious minds gazed at the sun, as it sank behind the Blue Ridge and wondered what lay beyond.

To the west, always to the west, lay the romance of unknown American lands and new adventure.

CHAPTER 12

The Finding of Manhattan
and New England

T HE ISLAND where the Indians of "Manna-hata" lived lies in a large and beautiful harbor, at the mouth of a mighty and beautiful river, which we know as the Hudson. Manhattan, its Upper Bay, and its rivers were not discovered by early explorers, because all three were almost completely hidden from passing ships by the forests of Long Island, Staten Island, and other smaller islands.

If the first explorers had come closer inshore, they might have found the future site of New York City much earlier, in spite of the islands that masked it. There would, however, have been nothing special to distinguish it. To the early explorers, it would have looked like just another island, though, as sailors, they would have seen the beauty and value of New York Harbor. On the island where the skyscrapers of Manhattan tower today, however, there was nothing special to be seen. This was just another wooded island with a few Indian villages, lying among other islands much like it.

There was a good reason why the sea captains who first sailed along the American coast stayed well out to sea. In those strange and uncharted waters, the first sailors had to navigate carefully, lest they run on rocks or shoals, hidden just beneath the surface. It was the same danger that had worried Cartier. They dared not risk damage to their ships, so far from home. There was no shipyard for repairs. There was no possible chance of help from other passing ships. Wisely, the captains "played it safe," and kept their vessels well off the unknown American coast.

There was another reason for keeping out to sea and sailing swiftly by. The sailing ships of those early days were rather clumsy craft. Unlike later sailing vessels, they could not sail easily into the wind. As a result, when they had a favorable wind, they kept right on sailing in one direction, as long as the fair wind lasted. Since they never knew how soon the wind would change, they did not pause to examine the country and describe it in detail, unless something very remarkable indeed attracted their attention.

Then, too, these men were not particularly concerned with the coasts past which they sailed or the lands that lay behind the coasts. They were still looking for Columbus's goal—a way to India and China. Everyone still believed that somewhere there must be a passage, leading through North America, to the Pacific Ocean. Intent on this, sailors ignored many things that might otherwise have led them to pause for exploration, on land.

The earliest description of our North Atlantic coast is that of Giovanni da Verrazano, who was sent out by Francis I, king of France. Verrazano reached North America somewhere near North Carolina in the spring of 1524, thirty-two years after Columbus. Thence he followed the coast northward all the way to Maine. If he had gone only a little farther, he would have discovered the St. Lawrence River before Cartier.

North America gave him a pleasant welcome, for, as his ship approached, the crew sniffed sweet and pleasant odors, blowing out from the land. In those days, when millions of wild flowers bloomed all at once in American forests, the whole Atlantic shore sent fragrance far out to sea, on a land breeze. Judging by the time of his arrival, Verrazano probably smelled the Southern magnolias. Many of the early explorers comment on this wave of perfume, which sometimes rolled out from the incredible mass of flowering trees, shrubs, and plants, each spring, when the American wilderness burst into blossom. One of the later voyagers said the air around him smelled as if he were in a flower garden, instead of on a ship at sea. Captain John Smith had a similar experience in the West Indies, and found much the same thing in America. Michael Drayton, one of Shakespeare's contemporaries, even wrote a poem about "the luscious smell of that delicious land."

As the ship passed what is now New York, some keen-eyed sailor noticed an opening. Verrazano put in with his ship and found one of the finest harbors in the world. Soon he was riding at anchor in the Upper Bay. He and his crew were the first white men to see Manhattan Island. They arrived seventy-five years before Henry Hudson.

Somewhere in New York Harbor, Verrazano went ashore, very likely on Manhattan Island itself. Wearing "the feathers of birds of various colors," the local Indians swarmed down to the shore to give him a friendly greeting. They seem to have felt no fear and to have shown no sign of hostility. They even pointed out a good place to land. Presently thirty canoe loads of other Indians came paddling over "from one shore"—Verrazano does not say which one. The white men saw the Hudson, "a very great river, which was deep in the mouth," and apparently entered it in a small boat, though they cannot have gone more than a very short distance upstream.

This first visit of the white men to Manhattan did not amount to much. Seeing that a gale was brewing, Verrazano hurried back to his ship. There is one curious passage in his note on the voyage: As he looked back at New York, where land is more expensive now than anywhere else in the world, he jotted down that "it was not without some properties of value."

Because he stayed so short a time, his visit seems to have made little impression on the Indians. When Henry Hudson came, seventy-five years later, there was not even a lingering tradition of the first white man's coming.

Verrazano sailed on past the Connecticut coast and along the Rhode Island shore, passing Block Island and anchoring in Narragansett Bay. The country around Newport, which has since become such a fashionable summering place, fascinated Verrazano and his men. They stayed two weeks, making friends with the local Indians and admiring the younger squaws, "of comely mien and agreeable aspect." Traveling as much as eighteen miles inland, quite unmolested by the natives, they found wide, fertile fields, with flourishing crops, plums, nuts which they called "filberts" (probably beechnuts or hazelnuts), apples, and other fruits they could not identify. Not all the clearings were for crops. The Rhode Island Indians had a reputation as the best farmers on the Atlantic seaboard, but they also knew that deer like to graze in clearings with young trees and green shoots sprouting from old stumps. They kept the trees cut down in some areas, simply to attract the deer. Otherwise, all New England was thick forest.

Though the New York and Rhode Island Indians had been friendly, the Indians in Maine would not allow the whites even to visit their villages. They were afraid of white men, possibly because they had been abused by wandering fishermen who left no record. Though they wanted to trade for the white men's goods, they would do so only by lowering bundles of their own goods down over the rocky Maine cliffs, to the ship's small boats, waiting below. From the white men, they wanted knives, fishhooks, and various metal objects, which they hauled up on their ropes, without ever coming near Verrazano's crew.

Sailing on northward along the coast, Verrazano admired the lovely islands off the coast of Maine, which are still favorite American vacation spots. Then, after passing a little way beyond what is now the Canadian border, he turned out to sea, toward Europe and home. Very little is known of the rest of his life, though it is believed he made one more voyage, during which he was killed by the Indians.

No more visitors are recorded on the New England coast until 1602, though there must have been French, English and Basque fishermen, from time to time. The waters of the St. Lawrence and of Newfoundland had now been fished for a century. A few venturesome fishermen must certainly have tried their luck in the teeming waters farther south. And indeed, though records are lacking, there is little doubt that this happened. The attitude of the Maine Indians toward Verrazano would be sufficient evidence of that, but there is more and better evidence.

As Bartholomew Gosnold, the first skipper to sail straight across the

Atlantic from Europe to New England, drew in toward the southern coast of Maine, in 1602, he beheld "a Biscay shallop with sails and oars," approaching. Naturally supposing the men in it were white, he hove to. To his amazement, the craft was entirely manned by Indians. One was wearing blue cloth breeches, another a waistcoat, breeches, stockings, shoes, and a hat. One or two others had a few things "made by Christians."

These Indians gave every sign of friendly feeling. They even knew a few "Christian words." But what were they doing with those clothes in that European shallop? It was plain enough that white men had recently met disaster upon that coast—shipwreck, massacre, robbery, or all three. The English newcomers cleared out immediately.

Though they took some notes on the appearance of the country, Gosnold and his men were not much interested in such matters. They had come for sassafras root, then in great demand in England as a medicine. The most fantastic virtues were attributed to tea made from this root. It was supposed to cure fever, stomach aches, and liver ailments—even to make people fat. Prices paid for it in London were so high that it was worth sending a ship all the way to America to get it.

Gosnold's records show that he must have been somewhere in Massachusetts Bay, inside the great "hook" of Cape Cod, which he named after making a mighty haul of codfish there. He went ashore—the first recorded landing in Massachusetts—and found the land covered with berry bushes of various sorts. What he called "whortleberries" may have been cranberries, which grow along the Masachusetts coast. More probably they were blueberries, still green. His crew found many strawberries, which Gosnold says were as sweet as those at home in England and much bigger. Wild strawberries today are very sweet but they are not nearly as large as cultivated berries. Probably wild strawberries today are smaller than they used to be, because they are now crowded out into the worst soil. Our cultivated berries are much larger than they were in Gosnold's day, for gardeners have been working to breed bigger ones for the last two centuries.

As Gosnold's crew rounded Cape Cod and coasted south, they found more open, grassy country along the shore. They gave Martha's Vineyard its name because of the immense quantities of grapevines on the island. There they saw great numbers of cranes, or herons, geese and other birds; but, from the names Gosnold gives, we cannot today tell what they were. The Englishmen no doubt saw the heath hen, a common bird in those days, now utterly extinct. It is too bad no one wrote down any description of the bird and its habits.

Sometimes Gosnold's sailors killed what they called "penguins." In this case, we know what Gosnold was talking about. There were no penguins on the New England coast. But the great auk was a large black and white bird, which a careless and untrained observer might mistake for a penguin. This tells us that the great auk—another bird now extinct, like the heath hen—once ranged south along the New England coast. It was one of the birds whose vast numbers had so amazed Cartier at the mouth of the St. Lawrence.

Gosnold had intended to start a permanent settlement on the island of Cuttyhunk in Buzzard's Bay, just south of Massachusetts. He had to give up this scheme because not enough men were willing to stay behind on that wild coast. The whole crew sailed back to England with their cargo of sassafras—and the first description of Massachusetts.

It is just possible that Cuttyhunk was the island Shakespeare was thinking about when he wrote "The Tempest." The best authorities, however, accept Bermuda as the original. But it is interesting to note that the Earl of Southampton was Gosnold's patron, as well as William Shakespeare's.

The next year, Massachusetts was visited by Martin Pring, a sea captain from Devonshire. A year or so later came the great French explorer, Samuel Champlain, then only at the beginning of a great career.

However threatening Verrazano may have found the Maine Indians eighty years earlier, Champlain and his Frenchmen found the natives friendly both in Maine and Massachusetts. It is true, there were one or two small skirmishes. But a new generation of red men had grown up since Verrazano's visit. They had seen enough of European fishermen to realize that it was worth while to welcome white men, not always for friendship's sake, perhaps, but for the metal knives and axes and other wonderful things they brought with them.

After Verrazano, seventy-five years passed before white men again appeared in the great empty harbor in which Manhattan Island lay, unless it is true that in 1525, one year after Verrazano, Estevan Gómez, a Portuguese in Spanish service, dropped anchor in the Bay. It is by no means certain he was ever there, and certainly neither his visit nor Verrazano's ever led to settlement.

When all this had long been forgotten, the Dutch hired an English captain, named Henry Hudson, "for to discover a Passage by the North Pole to China." Hudson tried in 1607 and failed. He tried again in 1608 and failed. In 1609, trying for the third time, he failed to find a way past the North Pole to China but he found something more important: He found New York. Or rather, he found it for the second time. And this time something was done about it. Hudson's Dutch employers were wiser than the men who had sent out Verrazano. They soon had the colony of New Amsterdam flourishing on Manhattan, though the English captured it from them in 1668 and renamed it New York.

On the morning of September 3, 1609, Hudson's little two-masted yacht, the *Half Moon*, came creeping into New York Harbor from the Lower Bay. Uncertain of these unknown waters, afraid of uncharted rocks and shoals like all these early seamen, Hudson kept a small boat moving ahead of his ship, taking soundings as it rowed, to make sure he would not ground in shallow water. He could feel the push of a strong current against the vessel's hull as he advanced, and correctly guessed that there must be a big river, somewhere on ahead. This might be the passage he had sought so long. He would push in and see. Verrazano, much less cautious, appears to have sailed right in.

This time, happily for us, we have the Indians' own version of the coming of the white men. Though Verrazano's visit had been forgotten, Hudson's made such an impression that the Indians were still talking about it 150 years afterward. Aged warriors told the story to a Moravian missionary, John Heckewelder. Though the story handed down from parents to children by many campfires was embroidered as the years went on, the tale checks fairly well with the day-to-day entries that one of Henry Hudson's officers wrote down on the spot. It checks also with a very early Dutch story, based on a conversation with Indians who were living when the *Half Moon* arrived, and which was later published. The tale preserves the red men's feeling of wonder, in that historic moment.

A few Indians were fishing from dugouts, "where the sea widens"—in other words, somewhere in the Lower Bay. Far out on the waves, they "spied at a great distance something remarkably large floating on the water, and such as they had never seen before." Paddling hastily back to shore, they called companions to see. More Indians came running down to the shore.

There it was, sure enough! Everyone could see the strange thing, but no one knew what it could be. Great was the speculation. Some thought it must be a large fish or other animal; some were of the opinion it must be a very large house. Whatever it might be, they could soon see that the queer thing was drawing closer.

It was time to warn other Indians scattered about in villages on the mainland and on the islands. Runners dashed over the forest trails. Canoes splashed hurriedly about the Bay. More Indians came rushing down to the shore. Black eyes in painted faces watched the Dutch ship come. Far down the Bay, something strange, something enormous to Indian eyes, was creeping over the surface of the water. At first it seemed dark with huge white wings. Then, as it drew closer, it appeared brightly colored with wings that seemed to grow ever whiter as the sunlight struck them.

There was no doubt that the strange object was moving toward them, and now it seemed to be a large canoe or house, but so large and so magnificent that only a god of some sort could possibly inhabit it. Perhaps the Great Spirit, the Master of Life himself, was coming to visit his red children. In that case, what to do? How should red men receive visiting divinity?

A council of chiefs met hastily. Nothing like this had ever happened before, and the strange object was steadily drawing nearer. While medicine men conjured hastily and squaws prepared a feast, the chief decided the best thing to do was to commence dancing. A dance was a religious ceremonial, sure to be appropriate to almost any great occasion.

As the dance commenced, more messengers came rushing to the

council with news. The strange thing was indeed a floating house of various colors—Dutch ships of the *Half Moon*'s time were gaily adorned. Whether it carried a god or not, it was now easy to see that it was full of living beings. More runners brought more news. These creatures were very strange indeed. The watcher on the shore could now see that they were of quite a different color from the Indians. Their dress was also odd. One was brilliant red all over—that must be the god himself. It was, in fact, Captain Henry Hudson in formal uniform: a gold-laced red coat.

As the floating house drew nearer, the Indians could hear the strange creatures on it, shouting across the water to them in a strange language. No one knew what they said, but the Indians shouted back. It seemed only good manners. Some of them wanted to run for safety into the woods. Others feared this might offend the newcomers, who would then surely seek them out and kill them. Better to stand their ground and see what was to come.

Seen close at hand, the floating "house" began to appear more and more like a large canoe. Finally it halted, its white wings flapping strangely. Then a small canoe put off. Old New York tradition says that Henry Hudson first stepped on shore at Coney Island, opposite Gravesend, Long Island. He was all in red and his clothing glittered in a way the Indians could not understand. Hudson had, in other words, gotten out his best clothes for the occasion and his gold lace shone in the sunlight.

As the Indians watched, a large "hockhack" as they called a gourd —in other words, a bottle—was brought to the red-clothed god by one of his servants. From it he poured a strange fluid of which he drank, and which he then offered to the serious Indian chief, who sniffed it cautiously. The Indians were afraid to drink, until one bold warrior tasted the proffered mysterious liquid. He fell at once to the ground, says legend, but presently arose to declare that nothing had ever given him such a feeling of happiness as the strange fluid. They all tried it and friendship was thus established between Captain Henry Hudson and the red men of "Manna-hata."

This was the tale told in the wigwams and around the campfires from father to son for many generations.

But the story was a little different according to the day-by-day log-book of Robert Juet, an English officer on the Dutch ship. (The commander's own log of the voyage has been lost.)

According to Juet, Hudson had again failed to find the long-sought passage. He had then cruised down the coast as far as "King's River in Virginia, where our Englishmen are." He did not know his friend, Captain John Smith, who had furnished information for Hudson's voyage, was there. If he had known, he might have stopped. Instead, he turned around and started north again, for a more careful examination of the coast. Probably he would have moved a great deal faster, if he had known how close Champlain had just come to discovering the Hudson River!

As the *Half Moon* came up the New Jersey coast in the early morning, the crew saw the light of a great fire, but no land. At dawn they saw Sandy Hook "all like broken islands," and eventually came into "a great lake of water," where they felt the current of a great river pouring seaward. When they anchored down the Bay about five in the afternoon, they could see the high hills toward the north—highlands on the Jersey shore and Harbor Hill on Long Island. When the mists cleared about ten o'clock on the morning of September third, Hudson sent a small boat ahead to take soundings while the *Half Moon* crept cautiously in. As they went, the sailors noted many "very great" fish. When they went ashore, a little later, they caught one so big it took four men to carry it aboard the *Half Moon*.

Juet does not mention the Indians' excitement. Naturally the men on the ship could have no idea of the amazement their incoming ship was causing among the Indians on shore. But Juet does remark that they came aboard later; that they seemed glad to see the white men; and that they brought green tobacco, which they gladly exchanged for knives and beads.

After making friends with the Indians, Hudson worked the *Half Moon* slowly up the river, doing a great deal of sounding as he went. When the tide came in each day, Hudson went with it a little farther. (The Indians, who did not understand tides, thought the river flowed both ways.) Sometimes, when the ship anchored for the night, Indians brought them beans and, while they were near salt water, very good oysters. At other times the men seined for fish, catching species like sturgeon and salmon which are no longer found in the Hudson.

As the ship went on, the men observed that the land was growing high and mountainous. About the fourteenth, they passed West Point. Four days later, they had arrived at the future site of Albany; and it was here, not at Manhattan, according to Juet, that Hudson gave wine to the Indians. This was Mohawk country, so that Hudson must have been making friends with the Mohawks just about the time Champlain was fighting them.

After a visit of several days, the white visitors started back down the river, admiring the great forests on each bank. They knew some of the species and commented on the large number of "trees of sweet wood." This was certainly the American sassafras, which is likely to grow in groves, or at least large clusters of the same tree. Chestnuts were already ripening and sailors gathered a great store of them to relieve the monotony of the ship's diet. Hudson and his men thought this as pleasant a land as they had ever seen and "the finest for cultivation."

The abundance of food made New York, the Hudson Valley, and indeed the whole American coast seem delightful to the *Half Moon*'s crew. Off the Maine coast, they had caught 130 lobsters in three days— that is, more than six lobsters apiece for a crew of twenty. The abundance of big fish continued along the coast and all the way up the Hudson. Even whales went up the river as far as Albany, though Hudson's men probably did not see any. Hudson River sturgeon might be seven feet long. Along the shores of New York Harbor and Long Island Sound, oysters, clams, lobsters, crabs could be had for the gathering; and this was true all along the coast down which they had come, though Hudson's men rarely stopped to find out. Since there were only a few Indians to catch them, these shellfish grew to enormous sizes. Later, one hears of oysters a foot long.

Though Hudson's men do not seem to have done any hunting, they could have killed deer, black bear, and an occasional moose on the Jersey shore, along the Hudson, or on the Connecticut coast. Streams and marshes were full of muskrats, which some of the first white men thought very good roasted and which are still sometimes eaten. Connecticut streams were filled with beaver dams. Beaver skins were worth a great deal of money in Europe. In America, stitched together, they made good warm robes, and beaver tails were excellent eating. But Hudson's men were on shore too briefly to discover many of these animals.

Small as Manhattan Island was, it had many brooks of clear, fresh water, which made its landscapes especially attractive. Strange to say, some of these brooks are still there, though now they flow through New York City in dark tunnels, underground. The only exception is in Washington Square, where a big apartment hotel has brought the water of one brook back to the light of day, to trickle through its lobby.

Wild flowers were so fragrant that a Dutch visitor, walking down the island with a companion, halted to enjoy the sweet smell, rising from the ground. Birds hovered everywhere. Early white visitors commented on the special abundance of many kinds of songbirds. Wild turkeys, geese, snipe, grouse—there was no end to the abundance of wild life. Manhattan's natural fruits were mulberries, grapes, persimmons, huckleberries, cranberries, and strawberries.

After spending a month on his river, on October 4 Hudson headed the *Half Moon* out to sea, on her way back to Europe. He sailed again the next year and discovered the great bay in Canada that bears his name. This time his crew suffered severe hardships and were frozen in throughout the winter. In the spring of 1611 mutinous sailors, led by the mate Robert Juet, the same who had been on the New York voyage, seized the great explorer and set him adrift in a small boat. He vanished from all human record on June 23, 1611.

With every ship returning from the New World, stories of that marvelous land continued to spread. The magnificent forests, the mighty trees, the wealth of fish and game, the immense rivers, the strange red people roused interest everywhere. Tales went from mouth to mouth in streets, homes, courts, and taverns. Some thought of the freedom such a land could give.

The English had already been in Virginia when Hudson came. Only eleven years after Hudson had gone, a band of exiles moored their bark on the New England coast and came ashore on a big rock in Plymouth harbor. They were the Pilgrim Fathers, who had come determined to live in this new land and call it home.

Still the curious minds of other men turned westward. What lay behind the coasts? Was there a sea passage through the new land? How far away was the Western Sea?

CHAPTER 13

Into Pennsylvania

VERRAZANO AND HUDSON had not attempted to explore Delaware Bay. Probably they were afraid of its many shallows and sandbars. When the Dutch first came to America, they, too, avoided sailing the Delaware, and settled on Manhattan Island, which they called New Netherland and later New Amsterdam. A few of them eventually did settle on the Delaware's east bank, about opposite the present city of Philadelphia. The Dutch village on Manhattan soon grew into a flourishing colony, under the leadership of Peter Minuit, the director-general. It was he who originally bought the island from the Indians for trinkets worth twenty-four dollars.

In spite of the dangers of the Delaware Bay and River, both English and Dutch soon began to explore them. About ten years after the Pilgrim Fathers had landed on Plymouth Rock, some unknown English adventurer made the first voyage up the river.

Indians killed him and all his crew. No one has any idea today who these Englishmen were. Neither does anyone know exactly what happened—or when. After the Dutch began to occupy more of the Delaware country in 1631, they found some of the Indians still wearing jackets of English make. In 1632, a squaw told them of the massacre. Except for that, no one, to this day, would ever have known it happened.

The Dutch now started a new village at a place they named Swanendael, near what is now Lewes, Delaware, on the west shore of the Bay. They brought horses and cattle with them, as well as brick enough to build a house, which they surrounded with a palisade. Here the settlers hoped to enrich themselves by whaling. They knew there were whales in Delaware Bay, and whale oil was bringing high prices, at home in Holland.

Like the Virginia settlers, these newcomers also found that, while they were still at sea, they could scent the new land before they could see it. Though they arrived as late in the year as December, they eagerly "smelt the land, which gave a sweet perfume, as the wind came from the northeast, which blew off land, and caused these sweet odors."

At that season, this could not have been the fragrance of wild flowers. A Dutch writer of the time explains that the fragrance "comes from the Indians setting fire, at this time of year, to the woods and thickets in order to hunt; and the land is full of sweet-smelling herbs, as sassafras which has a sweet smell." Burning cedars, too, are said to have given off a pleasant aroma.

No one knows much about this Dutch settlement, because it soon ended in tragedy. The ship that had brought the settlers sailed back to Holland. When it returned the next year, its sailors found a horrible spectacle. Indian raiders had wiped out Swanendael completely. Human skulls and bones lay about. There were also skulls of cows and horses, but not many of their bones. The Indians had apparently carried beef and horse meat away with them, taking bones and all.

About this time, the men in charge of the Dutch settlement on Manhattan Island made a bad mistake. They dismissed Peter Minuit, who had done so much to develop their colony. Minuit immediately offered his services to Sweden, for he knew that the Swedes, too, had for several years been planning to colonize in America. Before long, the Dutchmen were startled to find a Swedish colony on the Delaware, a location which they still claimed, even if they had not permanently settled it.

Peter Minuit guided his new employers, the Swedes, into Delaware Bay in April, 1638. They settled at Minqua Kill (that is, Minqua Brook), now Wilmington, Delaware. Here they built Fort Christina, named in honor of the Swedish queen. When the Dutch colony sent word that they must go, the Swedes paid absolutely no attention. Before long Dutch and Swedes were fighting; but neither side really won, for the British soon captured New Amsterdam and also took over the Swedish colony.

Then came William Penn and the Quakers. In 1680, Penn had bought land in eastern New Jersey to found a Quaker colony near another, which had been founded a few years earlier in the western part of the State. On January 5, 1681, King Charles II of England granted him Pennsylvania. Penn immediately began his new colony on a basis of complete religious freedom. He had established it for his fellow Quakers but he also admitted German religious sects and any one else who felt himself persecuted for religion's sake. Slowly, as white civilization spread north and west, from the first settlements along Delaware River and Bay, Pennsylvanians began to discover how much King Charles had given them.

Food was plentiful everywhere. Colonists in the southeastern part of the state quickly found the farming land fertile. But they did not have to farm for food. It was easy to shoot wild turkeys, weighing from thirty to thirty-six pounds—not particularly large for North America, where turkeys of fifty and sixty pounds are sometimes reported. Allowing for hunters' exaggeration, no one can doubt that some of the birds were very big indeed. The birds were easy to shoot because they were so tame. Some travelers in Pennsylvania met them running along the trails, and as late as the early 1800's, whole flocks appeared on the roads near modern Shippensburg. Quail, grouse, and passenger pigeons were everywhere.

Another abundant game bird, now a rarity, was the woodcock, which haunted swampy ground. These birds are fewer now, because so much swampy ground has been drained. However delicious a tidbit the woodcock might provide for dinner, white men soon found that where woodcocks most abounded, there was malaria, too. The scientific reason for this was unknown till our own day. The woodcock likes swamps. Where there are swamps, there are mosquitoes. Mosquitoes carry malaria. Very early settlers thought the site of Easton, on the Delaware, particularly healthy. It was free "from the fevers of the country from the fact of there being no woodcock ground within five miles."

The spring and autumn migrations brought huge flocks of wild geese, ducks, and swans. They paused briefly in Pennsylvania, then went on south, "with great cries, and hopping along with an almost incredible swiftness."

The whole Delaware Valley abounded with beaver, otter, and other animals, whose fur brought good prices in Europe. Deer were plentiful here as everywhere. "Hunter John" McHenry, who lived near Benton not far from the Susquehanna, used to sell venison in Philadelphia. He killed so many deer that the pile of antlers outside his cabin was as high as the roof. Elk and moose in those days came as far South as Pennsylvania. Now you must go far north to see such animals.

Though Pennsylvania never developed a whaling industry, there were plenty of whales to be seen near it. One party, traveling up the Delaware, saw two whales in the Bay, one more at the river's mouth, and a fourth whale, spouting in fresh water, near Wilmington.

Primitive Pennsylvania had buffalo, too. This was the "woods buffalo," not identical with the animal of the plains but closely related to it. They moved in herds of hundreds at a time. They seemed enormous to the first Pennsylvania settlers, though they were small indeed compared to the vast herds white men would encounter later, on the western plains.

The woods buffalo ranged as far east as the Susquehanna, perhaps even farther. One group of Pennsylvania hunters killed six or seven hundred in two years, taking only the skins and leaving hundreds of tons of beef to rot. As late as 1799 a herd of four hundred raided the hay fields near Selinsgrove, on the Susquehanna.

Trout and shad were plentiful, though at that time there were no bass, which the white man introduced to Pennsylvania streams much later. There were so many shad that a single haul of the net might bring in one to six hundred. Little boys of those early white settlements had a wonderful time, fishing in streams that had bigger fish, and more of them, than any fisherman will ever find again. Small Indian boys went fishing till they were old enough to learn a grown-up warrior's way. After that, they did more hunting than fishing. All Indian children lived a happy life, full of outdoor fun. It is no wonder that little white boys, after having been captives of the Indians, were sometimes reluctant to be rescued. Some of them grew to prefer Indian life—without any school or any household chores—to the white man's ways.

Three American animals always surprised the early explorers. These were the opossum, which had astonished the Spaniards in Florida, the flying squirrel, and the skunk. The flying squirrel seemed to them a remarkable creature. There are squirrels in Europe, of course, but the American flying squirrel glides through the air for long distances, partly supported by flaps of skin between its fore and hind legs. The European newcomers marveled greatly. The biggest surprise of all— and an unpleasant surprise—was the skunk. Many a white hunter got into serious trouble, the first time he tried to disturb the pretty little black-and-white animal, which seemed to him so tame and harmless!

Equally surprising was the ruby-throated hummingbird. It was a long time before any one discovered that it lives on the nectar of flowers, like a bee. One of the first ideas was that it must live on air, since it was never seen eating anything else.

An English traveler was much impressed—and even a little alarmed —the summer night when he first saw fireflies. They looked to him like sparks, dangerously close to dry hay, straw, and wood. He was afraid they might set something on fire.

There were no honey bees in America, until the white men brought them in. Many of their swarms escaped to the woods, where black bears soon learned to rob bee trees for their honey. The time came when the Indians began to regard the honey bees with dread, but not because of their stings. They called the bee the "white man's fly." They had learned that swarms of bees in the forest meant that white invaders were penetrating deeper into Indian country. Usually the honey bees were just about a hundred miles in advance of the line of white civilization.

Travel overland between the Delaware and the Hudson was difficult. For half a century after the first white men came to the Delaware, there was nothing but a path, for men and horses, which ran through an oak and hickory forest, in which were a few chestnuts, and more shrubby undergrowth than usual. If travelers passed the Falls of the Delaware, they were usually disappointed. The thunder of falling water impressed Europeans, few of whom had seen anything like it at home. But the "falls" near Trenton were really only a two-mile stretch of rapids, swift water running over a bed of stones. Passaic Falls, however, made a great impression.

Beginning with William Penn, Pennsylvania at first treated the Indians fairly. Though he held a charter from the English king, Penn knew that the land he had been granted really belonged to the Indians. Therefore he made friends with them and bought the land honestly. So long as he lived, the utmost friendliness prevailed between the red men and the white settlers of "Penn's Woods." They called him "Onas," which meant "Feather," and also "Pen," because in those days pens were made from goose feathers.

Even after William Penn's death, the Indians for a time remained friendly. The settlers near Reading were startled one day when a band of Indians, painted for war, suddenly appeared. But it turned out they had heard their white friends were in some kind of danger and had hurried to protect them.

Eventually, however, the Indians became less peaceful, as the Pennsylvanians slowly crowded them out of their land. They specially resented the "Walking Purchase," which was arranged by William Penn's successors. The Indians had agreed to sell land as far as a man could walk in a day and a half. The Indians were thinking of a real walk at ordinary speed. They never dreamed that the heirs of their old friend Onas would prepare for the "walk," by clearing a specially made path through the woods, and then send out specially trained athletes on a kind of marathon race. As a result, the whites were able to claim more of the treasured hunting grounds than the Indians had ever meant to part with. In revenge, the cheated redskins murdered the entire family of the fastest "walker," though they never caught the man himself.

The nearest large river valley to the west was obviously the next place for Pennsylvania settlement. This was the Susquehanna Valley, which was almost unknown until the middle of the eighteenth century. The first white man to travel the whole length of the river had been Étienne Brulé, Champlain's lieutenant. He wrote no descriptions whatever, but just told Champlain what he had seen on that journey in 1615. At about the same time, Captain John Smith, sailing along the coast, had found the river's mouth but had gone only a little way upstream.

The first descriptions of the unspoiled valley—which even to this day is as beautiful, in its way, as a smaller Rhine—come from the Indian agent and interpreter, Conrad Weiser, and from Moravian missionaries, who sometimes traveled along the river.

Weiser was one of the remarkable men of his time. Son of a German immigrant to New York, he had come with other Germans down the Susquehanna to settle in Pennsylvania. Pious, gentle, utterly fearless, skilled in the woods, Conrad Weiser had lived among the Iroquois as a boy. Thus he had acquired a shrewd knowledge of Indians' ways of thinking, as well as of their speech. He could speak all six of the Iroquois dialects and other native languages. On one occasion, when Iroquois and Nanticoke Indians held a council and could not understand each other, Weiser obligingly translated from one Indian tongue into another. He was a valuable agent, both for the Penns and for the Iroquois as well. The latter, who trusted him completely, seem to have thought Weiser was as much their agent as the Penns'.

His description of the Susquehanna and the wild mountains west of it, after his adventurous winter journey to the Iroquois country in 1737, is the first real account of this area that has been preserved.

The Susquehanna is really two rivers, which join to make a huge capital "Y," running from New York State to Chesapeake Bay. Into the lower part of the "Y" the Juniata flows from the west—still the most beautiful river in Pennsylvania and, in Indian times, the best hunting ground.

The waters of the two branches come together at modern Sunbury, which was known to the Indians as Shamokin. To control Shamokin was to dominate canoe routes and trails along three big rivers, controlling the very heart of Pennsylvania.

All this was perfectly clear to the shrewd sachems of the Iroquois League at Onondaga. Slowly they gathered in the conquered and tributary tribes—Shawnee, Tutelo, Sapony, Delaware, and Nanticoke —along the North Branch. Here they forced them to settle in the area around the site of modern Wilkes-Barre, then called Wyoming or Wajomink. Down the river at Shamokin, or near it, dwelt the Iroquois representative (or "half-king") Shikellamy. Another "half-king" represented the dominant Iroquois near Pittsburgh, to control western Pennsylvania and Ohio. White men in charge of their settlements' affairs had to deal either directly with Shikellamy in matters of less importance or, in great affairs of state, with the supreme Iroquois council at Onondaga—that is, Syracuse, New York.

In mid-winter of 1736, the Penns in Philadelphia had certain matters to lay before their friends, the Iroquois Council. In the whole colony, there was only one man to send. No one else spoke the various difficult Iroquois dialects so well as he. No one else understood so well the workings of the Indians' minds.

Between Shamokin and Onondaga lay a wilderness so thick that in many parts even game animals shunned it. Except at Wyoming, the Indian villages were far apart; and, in winter, the Indians were so near starvation themselves, that they could do little to help a traveler. There was often a good deal of game along the river, but not enough to ensure a winter's food supply.

Weiser set off, in February of 1737, on the long walk from Philadelphia to Onondaga. From the beginning it was a hard journey. The path over the mountains to Shamokin was almost impassable. He made a dangerous crossing of the flooded river, full of floating ice, which threatened at every moment to crush the frail canoe of an Indian who ferried him across. Going up the West Branch of the Susquehanna a short distance to the village where Shikellamy was then living, he found the chief absent and the Indians themselves almost without provisions. Iroquois warriors, arriving from New York, brought news that the snow was six feet deep in the mountains ahead. The Indians sold Weiser a little corn meal and some beans.

Shikellamy returned soon afterward, and at the same time an Iroquois warrior came limping in. He had gone to Virginia with a war party, which had found the southern Indians too much for them, and was now trying to get home alone, very much the worse for wear. With this warrior, Shikellamy, and two other companions, Weiser started off up the West Branch. Once they passed the remains of ancient earthworks, obviously fortifications, but very old. Even the Indians had no idea who had built them.

The small tributary creeks were so flooded that Weiser's men could hardly cross. The snow was already three feet deep. As they turned off from the main stream up Lycoming Creek, they had to scramble between "frightfully high mountains and rocks" overgrown with trees, in a valley no broader than the bed of the stream itself. In dismay, Weiser proposed returning. But, when the Indians insisted that the trail would soon improve, they scrambled onward, the red men climbing on hands and feet along the cliffs, above the rushing creek, while Weiser used a small hatchet to cut footholds in the ice. When the path crossed the icy stream, they had to wade. Then, because of the heavy growth, they had to move so slowly that their toes, in their dripping moccasins, were in danger of freezing.

The evergreen forests were so dense that the travelers could catch only an occasional glimpse of the sun. Sometimes the trees were so thick that they could not see twenty feet ahead. This was such difficult going that it took three hours to cover about a mile. They slept on evergreen boughs, laid on the snow. Next morning, they found the fire, around which they had warmed themselves the night before, had melted the snow underneath and sunk down a full yard.

The Endless Mountains began to live up to the name that weary and disgusted Indians had given them. Even in summer, without snow and cold and freezing water, Lycoming Creek was a bad route. Today most of that country is a state forest reserve.

Weary of wading the freezing creek, Weiser and Shikellamy decided to leave the valley and try traveling on the mountain itself. The going there was not much better. Within a quarter of a mile, Shikellamy slipped, at a point where the mountainside was "steeper than the roof of a house." The stone he caught to support himself came loose, so that he slid to within a few feet of a hundred-foot precipice with pointed rocks below. Here his pack went around one side of a sapling while Shikellamy went around the other and, luckily for him, he was caught. There he hung till his companions rescued him. When they reached the valley again, the old Indian, looking up at the precipice, thanked "the great Lord and Creator of the world, that he had mercy on me, and wished me to continue to live longer."

From time to time the path cut across the creek and the travelers had to cut a long pole to which they held as they waded, waist deep. It was still so dark and gloomy in those big woods "that for a mile at a time we could not find a place of the size of a hand, where the sunshine could penetrate, even in the clearest day."

They passed through parts of these primitive Pennsylvania woodlands where the dense growth of trees shut off the light so completely that small bushes and underbrush could not grow at all. This should have made travel easier. But instead of one obstacle, there was another. Thousands of rotting fallen tree trunks lay everywhere. Each step the traveler took was uncertain.

Forests like this had a strange effect. People who trudged along through the somber half-darkness, day after day, became quiet, scarcely speaking to each other. For no reason at all, they grew anxious, fearful, expecting danger at every moment. The gloomy half-light, unrelieved, subdued the spirits of travelers who could never see a bit of sky. Even game animals shunned those cold mountains in winter time to seek warmer quarters and better feeding grounds.

Weiser's small party had very little to eat on that miserable winter journey. A wretched and unappetizing diet of corn-meal gruel was all that kept them alive. At any other time of year, they would have found game birds, elk, and deer, as well as wolves and foxes, for the eastern forests were ordinarily filled with wild animals. As far east as the Susquehanna ranged the woods buffalo. In the northern part of the state there were moose.

The big woods—so still by day—in any time but winter were full of noises at night. The night-hunting animals on the prowl cried, shrieked, howled, and barked—panthers, wild cats, wolves, foxes—and the forest seemed alive with the hooting of many owls. But in mid-winter, the travelers felt the utter loneliness of the woods, forsaken even by wild creatures. No wonder these forests were called "The Shades of Death," a name Pennsylvanians often gave to very thick woodlands.

When Weiser and his group had finally struggled across Towanda Mountain and were descending Towanda Creek, travel began to improve. They emerged from the dismal forest of evergreens into a pleasant grove of white oaks. Though these were bare, gaunt, and leafless at that season, they made Weiser feel "as if we had escaped from hell." The wind grew warmer. They had dry ground to sleep on.

After one more desperate crossing of a flooded creek, and after eating their last reserve of food, they reached the North Branch of the Susquehanna. There they found the Indians were "hungry people, who sustained life with the juice of the sugar-trees," in other words, maple syrup.

When Weiser and Shikellamy at last reached an Indian village buried in the forest, they found the men were all out hunting, but so far had not been able to kill any meat. Though they had no meat, they did enjoy the luxury of corn, flavored with lye made of ashes. Many Indians liked this mixture—white men still use lye in making hominy. Some Indians thought that a little powdered woodash lent flavor to a meal. Others preferred the tart flavor of formic acid from insects, especially ants.

The country between Owego and Syracuse was also desperately hard going. There were mountains, swamps, thickets, cliffs against which the stream rushed closely, while such trail as there was wound back and forth across the streams, chilling the travelers in one ford after another. Not all places that looked like a possible path belonged to the real trail. In later years, one white traveler took what he thought was a trail, only to discover he was simply following the track of a black bear. Such a blunder would not be made with old Shikellamy along, even if the bears had not been hibernating. But Weiser emerged from the wintry mountains to describe them as "a dreadful thick wilderness," such as even he had never seen before. At one point, losing hope, he sat down to die, thinking that the bitter cold would hasten his end. Sturdy old Shikellamy, still vigorous after all their hardship, persuaded him to make one more effort and brought him safely to Onondaga.

As they came down out of the mountains on the north side, the heavy forest through which they had been traveling opened up into scattered groves. Though travel was far easier for the last forty miles, the party reached Onondaga in a state of exhaustion. The Iroquois received them hospitably and urged them to eat and rest, for "you look like Dead Men."

Weiser's return journey, after the winter was over, was much easier. His party in a canoe floated easily down the North Branch which was now clear of ice. There were almost no rapids to worry about, and the upper part of the river was so swift that, when the water was high, a canoe could run downstream at fifty miles a day. At this season, there was plenty of game. Weiser's party bagged a turkey and several wild ducks, though they spent little time hunting. They missed the only bear at which they got a shot.

They had no time for fishing, either, though the Susquehanna in those days was a fine stream for fish. The river, not yet contaminated by sewage and wastes from coal mines, was clear and beautifully transparent. They "might have seen a pin at the bottom," even where the water was chin-deep.

Difficult and dangerous though Weiser's mid-winter trip had been, his party was spared one seasonal hazard. The large numbers of rattlesnakes that later travelers saw in this part of the country were all hidden away, sleeping off the cold weather. In summer, one might see forty rattlers at a time, lying among the very rocks over which Weiser scrambled. Two white hunters later had to anchor their canoe in midstream, to get away from the snakes at night. Indians in the Susquehanna Valley sometimes slept in beds held above the ground on forked sticks, to keep the snakes from crawling into their warm blankets. The snakes were not trying to harm any one. They merely wanted to keep warm. But a man, stirring in his sleep, might roll on them and, if he did, was bitten.

Rattlers are peculiar to America. Before the white man came, they were rarely disturbed. Since the shrill note of their rattles warned of danger, it was easy for Indian hunters to avoid them. Though they were feared, they were highly esteemed by some tribes and even by some white men. The Cherokees and Hopis held them sacred. The Cherokees referred to the rattlesnakes in one sacred valley as "bright old inhabitants."

The snakes have always had a high medical reputation. A belt of rattlesnake skin was supposed to give a pregnant woman easy delivery of her baby. The American explorers, Lewis and Clark, gave a powder made of the ground rattles to Sacagawea, wife of their interpreter, hoping it would make the birth of her child easier. Some modern Americans highly esteem rattlesnake oil. In early days, the snakes were eaten only in emergencies. Not until our own times did there develop a market for canned rattlesnake meat.

From this Susquehanna country, exploration of western Pennsylvania turned into trails beside the beautiful "Blue Juniata." Along the river and its tributaries, these trails ran almost east and west till they reached the series of Allegheny ridges that bar Pittsburgh off from the rest of Pennsylvania. Crossing these mountains, they wound on through the forests to the rich Ohio Valley and the middle-western prairies.

As the traveler approached modern Bedford, Pennsylvania, the mountains grew steeper and higher. The dreaded Alleghenies were "impenetrable" thickets of scrub oak and laurel on the long, parallel mountain ridges which are characteristic of the Pennsylvania landscape in the extreme eastern and western parts of the state. They are old mountains, much eroded through endless geological time, without the towering, jagged peaks of the much younger Rockies. None of them were much more than half a mile high, but no woodsman then had any idea of the tremendous ranges that the western pioneers of the next century would have to cross. A traveler scrambling up one Allegheny ridge only to have to scramble up another just as bad, naturally thought them impenetrable. But in springtime, when the whole tangle of mountain laurel burst into bloom, even the weariest traveler had to admire the sight.

Near Pittsburgh, where the atmosphere was remarkably clear, there was a magnificent view from the Allegheny Ridge. At this place to-day one looks down only on the smoke and fume of roaring modern industry. Looking westward from this point in primitive times, one saw, stretching endlessly toward the horizon, only treetops, gently moving like a green sea, or tossing like the ocean after a great storm. This particular view became famous among early white settlers. Though probably the finest of its kind, it was typical of the Pennsylvania landscape almost anywhere. Exuberant descriptions written by early white explorers in this region say the beholder was "enchanted" by such views.

Amid this beautiful country, the site of the village of Pittsburgh stood out, with various Indian villages scattered about in its vicinity. Here, through forested hills, the clear waters of the Allegheny River, flowing from the north, meets the more turbid waters of the Monongahela coming from the south, and joins in the Ohio which flows, through rich forests which eventually become plains and savannahs, to the Mississippi.

Here, at last, was a waterway leading, if not to the west, at least to the southwest. Might it not be a way to the Western Sea?

Through this beautiful, unspoiled, wild country lying as it had lain since glacial times, unchanged, the first English explorers and traders struggled westward, while French explorers and traders were working their way south. Their paths crossed at Pittsburgh, and empires came to grips.

CHAPTER 14

La Salle Explores

WHILE WILLIAM PENN and his Quakers were settling Pennsylvania, the French were just beginning to make their way into what was later to become the Middle West. The first white discoverer to leave a record of the Ohio River country was Robert Cavelier, Sieur de La Salle, a recently ennobled Frenchman from Rouen. Educated by the Jesuits, he had come to Canada in 1666 to begin twenty years of exploration which took him from Canada to the Gulf of Mexico and led to his death at last, murdered by his own men, somewhere in Texas.

For two years after reaching Canada, La Salle lived the life of a pioneer on land granted him by the fathers of the order of St. Sulpice, of which his brother was a member. It was at the western end of the island on which Montreal stands. He occupied himself with farming, trading with the Indians and listening to their stories. The stories interested him more than anything else. Seneca warriors, wintering there, had told him about a stream that rose in their country—that is, western New York—and flowed into the sea at such a distance that it took eight or nine months to travel there. The Indians were thinking of the Allegheny, Ohio, and lower Mississippi as a single river.

The Canadians called La Salle's farm "La Chine," that is, "China," ridiculing his expressed hope of traveling from it to the Orient—and using it as a base for Chinese trade!

Eager to see the new country, La Salle secured permission to visit it in company with two Sulpitian missionary priests. With guides, the party proceeded in 1669 by canoe up the St. Lawrence, into Lake Ontario, and then overland to the Seneca village near the modern town of Victor, in western New York, where they hoped to find Indians who would show them the route into the new country.

At this moment, a Seneca war party returned, with a prisoner from one of the Ohio tribes. La Salle, thinking the captive would make a perfect guide, tried to buy him; but the Senecas preferred to have fun with him in their own grim way. The horrified white men had to sit by, while the prisoner was first burned alive, and then eaten.

Seeing there was no hope of help at this village, the party went on to another at the head of Lake Ontario. They heard the roar of Niagara in the distance. Indians told them the sound came from one of the most beautiful waterfalls in the world, which fell from a rock "higher than the highest pine"; but they were in too much of a hurry to go out of their way to look at it.

To their astonishment, another white man appeared at this Indian village. It was probably Louis Jolliet—later to be Father Marquette's companion on the Mississippi voyage—or perhaps Joliet's brother, on his way to examine Lake Superior copper deposits. The two priests in La Salle's party changing their plans, went off with Jolliet, leaving La Salle, as they thought, to go back to Montreal.

Instead, as soon as his companions were gone, La Salle started off to the Iroquois capital at Onondaga, where he apparently found an Indian who knew the Ohio country and was willing to go there with him. At the head of a small party, the determined Frenchman reached one of the upper tributaries of the Ohio, and moved down to certain "falls," by which he must have meant those at Louisville, Kentucky. Here his men deserted him, and he had to make his way back to Canada alone, living on wild plants, game, and chance gifts of food from passing Indians. He reached Canada in 1670, with a thrilling story to tell, but the journals and maps which recorded it seem to have vanished a hundred years later—lost by a careless owner.

Lacking these records, some historians have questioned whether La Salle really did discover the Ohio, though the great American historian, Francis Parkman, believed that he did. However that may be, there is no doubt that when La Salle went down the Mississippi in 1682, he really did see the Ohio, or at least its mouth. No one knows just where he was from 1670 to 1673. It is only known that he was hunting on the Ottawa River, before he returned to the Canadian settlements in 1670.

Though the papers in which La Salle told his own story have vanished, there are many descriptions of "the Ohio country" which, though of a little later date, give a picture of the unspoiled middle western wilderness he saw, as it was before the white man's blighting hand fell upon it.

The beauty of the primitive Ohio impressed all who saw it. Indeed, the French name, La Belle Rivière is supposed to have been merely a translation of the original Indian name, Ohio. La Salle says that "Ohio" is the Iroquois word and "Olighin-cipou" the Ottawa word, and that both mean "Beautiful River." There is no doubt that "cipou," or "sipi," was a common word for river in several Algonkian dialects.

An early traveler on the Ohio remarks that though scenery in some places on the Hudson and Connecticut and other rivers often equals anything on the Ohio, "its peculiarity is that it is *all* beautiful. There are no points bare of beauty." Its meandering course through forest glades "exhibited at every bend a change of scenery," and a "passage down the river was extremely entertaining." In spring the redbuds, or Judas trees, bursting with pink blooms, gleamed through the still bare branches of the forests; in autumn, the white bark of the sycamores accentuated the brilliant colored foliage. Kentucky cardinals with gay red plumage called to each other across the stream, and Carolina parroquets, red, green, and yellow, flashed among the trees.

Night and moonlight made the primitive Ohio lovelier still. One traveler commented upon the "constant shifting of the scene, the alternation of bright and dark sides of the hills, together with the variation in the appearance of the river—one place reflecting the beautiful beams of the moon, and another enveloped in the deep shadows cast from the lofty and overhanging bluffs—altogether form a scene surpassing in beauty and effect any thing else which I have seen."

These ravishing scenes were even more "entertaining" to the beholder because wild life was so abundant. "The flocks of wild geese and ducks which swarm upon the stream, the vast number of turkies, partridges, and quail we saw upon the shore, and the herds of deer or some other animals of the forest darting through the thickets afforded us constant amusement."

The story of La Salle's next venture into the unknown lands of the Middle West is preserved both in his own account and in that of Father Louis Hennepin, the missionary priest who accompanied him. Because he went, late in 1678, with an advance party some time ahead of La Salle, Father Hennepin is the first white man to leave a description of Niagara Falls, though Champlain had already written down what the Indians told him about it.

Father Hennepin exaggerated the height of the falls, saying they were five hundred feet high—later he made it "six hundred feet and more," though the actual height is 167 feet. The space under the falls was "big enough for four Coaches to drive a breast without being wet." He thought the spectacle "the most Beautiful, and at the same time most Frightful Cascade in the world." A modern geologist later excused Hennepin's exaggeration. It was no wonder, he said, that Hennepin, coming suddenly upon the falls which no European traveler had ever seen before, should have believed them to be twice their real height. Actually, he made them more than three times their real height.

Having admired the falls, Hennepin moved on, and was soon joined by La Salle, who set to work building a sailing vessel, the *Griffon,* above the falls. La Salle's trusted lieutenant was Henri Tonti, a soldier who had lost his right hand in a grenade explosion in the French Army. (It had been replaced with an artificial hand of iron, which he covered with a glove. Indians were amazed to find how hard Tonti could hit with his gloved hand.) Tonti directed the building of the little vessel while La Salle went off to the French settlements. By

August of 1679, the *Griffon* was under sail and La Salle had returned. The next month, La Salle's party sailed on to Green Bay, in Lake Michigan. Here he traded in furs, sent his ship and its cargo back to the settlements with Tonti, while he himself, with Father Hennepin and others, went down Lake Michigan in canoes.

It was a desperate journey. They ran so short of food that for a time each man had only a daily handful of dried corn. Finally they saw crows and eagles clustered around an object on the shore and, paddling over to investigate, came upon half of a very fat deer left there by wolves. The white men chased away the birds, and ate what remained of the venison.

After this the hunting improved. They lived on "staggs" which may have been deer, moose, or caribou, "a great many Turkey-Cocks very fat and big," and grapes as large as plums.

When they found the footprints of strange Indians, they stopped hunting, for fear the sound of shots might bring on an attack. But when one of the men could not resist letting drive at a treed bear, Fox Indians, hearing the report, made trouble at once. It was the kind of thing that worried all commanders in the big woods when game was so plentiful. In every column, trying to move stealthily through the woods, there was always some reckless soul who could not resist the perfect shot that was sure to be offered his itchy trigger finger sooner or later. This time, when the Indians found the French alert and ready for them, there was only a slight skirmish. Then they made friends, and the incident ended in "Dancing, Feasting, and Speeches."

By November, La Salle, Hennepin, and their party had reached the mouth of St. Joseph's River. La Salle paused to build a fort, near the modern town of St. Joseph's, Michigan.

The magnificent Michigan forests were thick. The flat-topped hill near the river's mouth which La Salle selected had to be cleared of its trees before building could even begin. It took hard work through all of November; and for three weeks there was nothing to eat, except bears which came down to the banks for the wild grapes. Though the men got tired of living on bear meat, bears were easy to get, and hunting them took little time. La Salle would allow no deer hunts till his fort was built.

Fortunately, Henri Tonti arrived on November 20 with two canoeloads of venison. But he also brought the dismal news that the *Griffon,* on which La Salle was depending for quick and easy communication with the Canadian settlements, was lost.

In spite of that there was no turning back. The party started up the chill waters of St. Joseph's River on December 3, looking for the portage that would take them over the watershed, into the Mississippi Basin. It is easy to paddle past a portage that leads from one wilderness lake or river to another, for a portage is only a narrow path, winding among thick-set trees and often obscured by the heavy underbrush along the shore. La Salle's men missed this one because their Mohican guide, whose quick eyes would have spotted it, happened to have gone ashore to hunt.

Realizing that they had lost their way, La Salle landed to look for the portage and got lost himself. That, too, is an easy misadventure in the big woods. It was especially easy for La Salle, because snow was falling and he could not see the sun. After missing his way he ran into a swamp, made a wide swing around it, and pushed ahead through snow and darkness—the worst thing he could have done. Both he and his men, waiting by the river, fired signal shots, but they were so far apart that neither heard the other.

About two in the morning, La Salle saw a fire and, certain that he had at last found his way back to camp, rushed up to it. There was no one beside the little wilderness campfire—only a pile of dry grass; but someone had been lying on it so recently that the impression of a human figure was plain and the grass was still warm. He had obviously frightened off a lone Indian hunter.

He shouted friendly messages in as many Indian languages as he knew; but when the silent, snow-muffled woods gave back no answer, he built a barricade of bushes, so that he would hear anyone approaching, lay down on the warm grass bed himself, and went to sleep—so tired that he was willing to risk his scalp.

Rested and clear-headed in the morning, he found his way safely back to camp, bringing with him two possums that he had clubbed while they swung by their tails from a limb. That night he and Father Hennepin were nearly burned to death when the dry reed mats of which their wigwam was made took fire.

Their Mohican guide, having found the portage, had come back before La Salle. They were off next morning, over a five-mile carry, from St. Joseph's River, across the height of land, to the Kankakee River and the Mississippi Basin. Starting somewhere near South Bend, Indiana, they paddled downstream through dull and unattractive land. The whole area was so marshy they could not explore the country back of the riverbanks.

In the low, flat Indiana and Illinois country, the rivers were often blocked by beaver dams and fallen trees. Behind these, water backed up, so that there were great stretches of marshes, ponds, and quagmires. For more than a hundred miles, they found not a single camp site that would have been dry enough to use, if the ground had not been frozen. This country has changed a good deal in modern times. In the last fifty years, most of these swamps, ponds, and marshes have been drained entirely. People who today see Indiana and Illinois find it hard to believe that these regions could have been so impassable.

As the party went farther into Illinois, the scenery changed. Ascending the low hills which now began to appear along the river, La Salle and his men could see rolling stretches of prairie ahead. These were dull green, even in winter.

From the Kankakee they passed into the Illinois River, flowing through flat country, which it frequently inundated. Its upper waters were full of beaver, whose silted-up ponds were probably the reason for many of the "terres tremblantes"—swamps of "trembling ground" —that made travel difficult. Beyond the marshes which often edged the banks, however, the canoeists saw "nothing but fine fields as far as you could see, broken here and there with groves of trees." The groves were the beginning of what later became known as "oak openings," or "orchards," that is, clusters of oaks standing near enough to be "a shady grove, but too distant to make a forest proper."

Passing modern Ottawa, Illinois, and Buffalo Rock, La Salle came at last to a big village of Illinois Indians, near the modern town of Utica.

Weary men at the paddles looked eagerly ahead. On their left towered a huge cliff—which they would later name Starved Rock—covered with forest. Along its edge, trees hung out over the river below. The river ahead slipped silently among wooded islands. Open, low-lying meadows swept back from its banks. On the dry spots in the plain, most of which was by this time marshy with winter floods, they could see about five hundred Indian lodges, each big enough to house several families.

These were not conical bark or skin tepees, but rounded structures of bent poles, with roofs shaped like a modern Quonset hut and covered with rush mats closely sewn together.

As the French canoes came nearer, La Salle was disappointed to find the village deserted. Normally, it would have been swarming with Indians, for each lodge was big enough for five or six fires, shared by families living in chambers on opposite sides. But as the French drew in toward shore, not a single smoke could be seen curling up from the long narrow vents. The whole village had gone buffalo hunting.

What were the white men to do? They were almost completely out of food. Looking about the empty village, they soon found the pits in which the Illinois, like other Indians, stored their corn. Now, robbing a cache is one of the high crimes of the wilderness. However great your own need, anything you take away may leave the rightful owner, who finds his reserve stores gone, in deadlier peril still. To this day, Royal Canadian Mounted Police are ready to prosecute any wilderness traveler who violates a lonely and unprotected wilderness cache, though owners are likely to be lenient when danger or hunger offers an excuse. After some hesitation, since there was still no game, La Salle decided, in view of his urgent need, to take thirty or forty bushels of corn, hoping to pay for it later with gifts.

There was much excitement a few days later when, in early January of 1680, they came suddenly upon the Illinois Indians' hunting camp. Though carefully avoiding any signs of hostility, La Salle made no signs of friendship either. The red men might mistake that for a trace of weakness. But when the Indians produced their peace pipe, he produced his own, and friendship was established. The matter of stolen corn was taken care of by gifts of steel axes, articles of priceless value to these Indians who almost never received white men's goods.

A little below modern Peoria, La Salle built Fort Crêvecoeur, or "Heartbreak." The name shows how he was beginning to feel about the discouragements of the explorer. Nevertheless, after his men had built a forty-foot keelboat from logs sawn by hand on the spot, he sent Father Hennepin and two men to explore the lower waters of the Illinois. La Salle himself went back, overland, to the French settlements, to get fresh supplies.

By the end of February, 1680, Father Hennepin was on his way. The travelers soon noted that the soil appeared "blackish" and the priest guessed, from its color, that it was fertile. He was right about that. He was just below the fertile state of Iowa, which today has one fourth of the Class A farm land in the United States. What he was seeing was the result of centuries of the slow rotting of prairie vegetation, made still more fertile by the "chips" dropped through the ages by millions of buffalo and fertilized at last with their bones. The country was a vast compost heap that nature had built up for centuries. No wonder that today it includes so much fine farm land.

They came safely to the Mississippi, but there they were captured by the Sioux. After a miserable captivity, they were rescued by the famous voyageur, Daniel du Luth, for whom the Minnesota city is named.

Many adventures befell the other group left under La Salle's heroic lieutenant, Henri Tonti, in the Illinois country, while the leader himself was in the French settlements; but they add no new information to what is known of the country, and La Salle's own last adventures in the South came after other white men—the Spaniards—had explored much of that country.

When La Salle came back to Fort Crêvecoeur in the autumn, a dreadful disappointment awaited him. The fort stood empty, a mere ruin. During his absence, an Iroquois war party had made the long journey from their own territory in New York, to make a surprise raid in the Illinois. The local Indians had been driven away. The faithful Tonti, wounded, had had to withdraw to Green Bay, in Wisconsin, on the western shore of Lake Michigan. He had reached there after a desperate journey with only five men, all he had left. On the trip they had lived on roots and such food as they could find in deserted Indian villages.

But disappointment could not stop Ferdinand La Salle. When he found Tonti at last, at Mackinac, they were soon deep in plans for new adventures. Back to the Illinois River they went, this time building their fort on the high cliff they had noticed on the first trip. When food ran short, it got its name, Starved Rock, but its height made it hard to attack. Hostile Indian war parties would have a weary climb before they even reached it. La Salle did his best to persuade friendly Indians to settle near it for protection in case the Iroquois raided them again.

Once the fort was secure, La Salle and Tonti started down the Mississippi. They reached the Gulf of Mexico in 1682 and claimed the entire valley for the French king, Louis XIV. It was they who named it, in his honor, Louisiana—a name which then applied to country hundreds of miles beyond the present state.

After this great achievement, La Salle soon found himself in trouble. In the very year when he had started down the Mississippi, his friend Frontenac was replaced as governor. The new governor was unfriendly. He sent La Salle orders to give up command of his fort on the Illinois and return to Quebec to answer for alleged wrongdoing. La Salle sent Tonti back to the fort to turn it over to the governor's new commander.

He calmly ignored the charges against himself. Instead of going to Quebec, he went straight on to France to report to the king himself. In Paris La Salle was received enthusiastically, and the king restored his command and all his honors.

La Salle was now sent back to America to establish an entirely new French colony at the mouth of the Mississippi, which he already claimed as French soil. Here, no governor could interfere with him. Here, he would not have to worry about orders from far-away French Canada. From Illinois to the borders of the Spanish colonies (which were extremely indefinite) La Salle was now authorized to command in the king's name. He sailed July 24, 1684, with four ships and two hundred colonists.

From the start, however, things went wrong. La Salle was a hard man to get along with, the kind of man who is more successful with a few friends in the wilderness than as the leader of a large command. He quarreled with the naval officer in charge of the ships. One of his ships was caught by pirates. Somehow, the three remaining ships sailed past the mouth of the Mississippi without seeing it, landing at last on the Texas coast, probably at Matagorda Bay far beyond the great river. La Salle must have thought this was the Mississippi mouth. At any rate, he started to erect a colony on what is now Lavaca Bay.

Only after the ships had sailed back to France (March 12, 1685) did La Salle discover his mistake. Realizing at last that he was nowhere near the Mississipi, he began to hunt for it, which was not easy. La Salle had no map. He had no idea which way the river lay or why they had ever missed it. Worst of all, while La Salle was away on these expeditions, the colonists became dissatisfied. Twice they plotted to kill him.

After two years, La Salle decided to give up Matagorda Bay. In January, 1687, nearly two years after the ships had gone home, taking all the colonists with him he started out to find the Mississippi and found a new colony. There was more grumbling, then downright mutiny. Finally on March 19, 1687, somewhere near modern Navasota, Texas, conspirators killed La Salle.

La Salle's brother Jean, a nephew, and Joutel were allowed to break away. After a long journey, they met some of Tonti's men in Arkansas and finally reached Tonti himself in Illinois. Not daring to tell him of La Salle's murder, they spent the following winter with him, then went on to Quebec. Not until September 1689 did Tonti learn that his friend La Salle was dead. He went South in December to try to find the colonists, but they had disappeared.

La Salle's work was over. He had been the first explorer to sail down the Mississippi to its mouth. Its great valley had been opened to white man's civilization.

Change would now follow. Pushing ever westward, white pioneers, coming to live on the great river's east bank, would be looking across to the country that stretched away to the setting sun and wonder: What was it like out there? How far to the Western Sea?

It was still a greater land than anyone imagined, a land dominated and cherished by Apache, Sioux, Blackfeet, Cheyenne, and many other tribes of red men living their lives as they had done for centuries of time.

CHAPTER 15

The Wild Middle West

LA SALLE'S seventeenth-century exploration of the
Middle West had been almost entirely along the rivers. He traveled
by land only in emergencies and of such trips left very little record.
Not until the next century have we any detailed descriptions of the
country as it looked to travelers passing overland through prairies
and "oak openings" of the middle western states, or through the forests
and meadows of Kentucky, on the south shore of the Ohio.

Both French and British eighteenth-century exploration of "the Ohio
country," which meant most of the Middle West east of the Mississippi, started from Pittsburgh. This was true whether they went by
canoe, on horseback or on foot.

Daniel Boone and his comrades moved into Kentucky from Virginia
and North Carolina, mostly through Cumberland Gap. Early travelers down the Ohio might land on the Kentucky shore; but few of
them went inland. In later years, hundreds of families came down
the Ohio.

It was unavoidable that French power, reaching southward from the St. Lawrence, and British power spreading westward from the Atlantic coast, should clash at Pittsburgh. Both French and English had been quick to see the strategic value of the great "Y" formed by the three rivers there—the Allegheny, the Monongahela, which joined to make the Ohio. This was the key to "the Ohio country." It might be the key to "the Illinois" (then understood to include Indiana and part of Missouri) which lay beyond. It was also one of the main routes to Kentucky.

The French, coming south from Lake Ontario and Lake Erie to this important area, recognized its beauty and future value. Jesuit missionaries—who traveled with French explorers in the North, as they traveled with Spaniards in the Southwest—left many records of their impressions of the country. On the south shore of Lake Erie they found lands "with very pretty prairies scattered among them, watered by rivers full of fish and beaver." The country produced a variety of fruits, nuts, game birds and animals. "The bears here," said one priest, "are fatter and taste better than the most savory pigs in France."

All the early European visitors found the land bountiful. Nor was this a matter of food and furs only. No one could fail to notice the country's general economic value. From the moment the French started down the Allegheny or the English up the Monongahela, it was "good rich country," everywhere. Huge trees, growing in thick forests, would provide abundant timber. Plainly, the ground was fertile. Clear it, and it would grow good crops. In Kentucky, where the French did little exploration, the first American "Long Hunters" found the land even more productive.

It is ironical that none of these early travelers guessed that the dirt beneath their feet in western Pennsylvania concealed wealth greater than anything else they saw. None of them ever lived to know that he had been walking over one of the most valuable coal and oil fields in the whole world. In the Europe and America of that day, coal and oil mattered not at all. People burned wood. Gasoline, and even coal oil, were not even thought of.

Occasional wanderers in the wilderness that concealed the oil fields of today sometimes saw "Seneca Oil"—crude petroleum—floating on streams or springs in New York, Ohio, and Pennsylvania. Occasionally, it seeped out on the ground. No one guessed how many uses the queer-smelling stuff had. No one dreamed that petroleum would one day be a matter of life and death to mighty nations, or that in two world wars our country would "float to victory on a sea of oil."

A few white men sometimes skimmed the strange fluid from the water on which it floated, because they thought it was good for their rheumatism. The Indians had long believed the oil had medicinal qualities.

The French had little to do with the beautiful country on the south bank of the Ohio, though voyageurs passing the Ohio River certainly landed on the Kentucky shore for a little hunting. It was one of those completely empty areas, of which there were several in primitive America. No Indians lived there. During the years just before the American Revolution, there were no villages of any tribe within what is now the state of Kentucky. It was, however, greatly valued as a hunting ground, for where no human beings lived, the game animals flourished and multiplied. Red hunting parties came regularly, hunted, and went home.

The first white men to visit Kentucky of whom we have any record were entirely English and American. The settlement of the state is associated in most people's minds with Daniel Boone—and rightly so; but Boone, though a great leader, was only one of many heroic American frontiersmen who risked their lives to open new country along the frontier.

A hundred years before Daniel Boone, at least one white man had crossed Kentucky from the Ohio River to Tennessee. This was Gabriel Arthur, who lived near Petersburg, Va. Captured by the Cherokees, he escaped torture. Soon he was on such friendly terms that he joined a Cherokee war party in a raid on the Shawnees. He was captured again. He made friends with the Shawnees too, and, by quick thinking, persuaded them to let him go. He showed the delighted warriors his steel hunting knife. The Shawnees had no iron implements of any kind. When they found that their prisoner knew where to get more of those wonderful steel knives, in exchange for nothing but beaver skins, they told him to go and get some. Arthur reached the Virginia settlements, June 18, 1674. He stayed there—and let the Shawnees wonder what had become of their knives! Arthur was probably the first white man to see so much of Kentucky, but like many first adventurers, he left no written account of what he had seen.

Between Arthur and Daniel Boone, a few other curious people pushed into Kentucky. Unknown Frenchmen are supposed to have gone south as far as Big Bone Lick—not very far below the Ohio. If they did, they found what Daniel Boone found later. Tusks of the mammoth, now extinct, lay all about. So did pieces of the back bones of the huge creature. Perhaps there were bones of other prehistoric creatures. The people who found the bones could not tell; but they recognized the long, curved ivory tusks of the mammoth. These lay either on the surface or near it.

The animals cannot, therefore, have been very ancient. There were no living mammoths when white men came into the country. It is just possible that they survived until about the time of Columbus, or one or two hundred years earlier. When hunters camped at Big Bone Lick they found that the huge vertebrae, with their hollow sides uppermost, made good camp seats.

In 1716, Governor Alexander Spotswood, of Virginia, had led a group of friends over the Blue Ridge and into the Shenandoah Valley; but they did not go beyond the western boundary of modern Virginia. In 1750, however, Dr. Thomas Walker, from Fredericksburg, passed through Cumberland Gap and into eastern Kentucky.

Not until the 1760's, however, did parties of "Long Hunters" and the Boone brothers, Daniel and Squire, begin the exploration of Kentucky's "dark and bloody ground," which eventually led to white settlements. The Long Hunters were so called because they left the settlements on long wilderness hunts that might last a year or more. Like the Boone brothers, they were chiefly in search of furs and deerskins, which commanded good prices. Usually one man served as "camp-keeper," staying in camp to cure the skins, while the others ranged the woods. When the long hunt was over at last, the skins and furs were brought back to the settlements on packhorses.

Daniel Boone's interest in Kentucky had been roused by John Finley, a trader who had been in Kentucky as early as 1767. He had traded with Indians along the Ohio, as far downstream as the falls, now

Louisville, and had gone south along the Kentucky River. Returning, filled with enthusiasm about "Kaintuck," he fascinated Daniel Boone with his stories of this wonderful hunting ground. In the spring of 1769 Finley, with Daniel and Squire Boone and their brother-in-law, John Stuart, and three camp-keepers, set off for this wonderful new land.

The forests were magnificent, but Kentucky was not all forests. In and around what is today Barren County, lay the "Barrens." They were so called, not because they were really barren, but because the land was open prairie, without forest. There was no sign that forests had ever grown there. The prairie was carpeted with grasses, wild rye, wild oats, and flowers. Here buffalo and elk grazed. The bleaching bones, horns, and skulls of others lay about. There was so much game in Kentucky and Tennessee that one hunter counted a thousand animals near a single salt lick. These were places where salt flavored the earth and game animals, crazed for salt, came in huge numbers. Of course a "thousand animals" story would only have amused a Sioux or Comanche who, in that mysterious land beyond the big river, might see a herd of a hundred thousand or more buffalo at a time, in the great plains and prairies farther west. But as yet few white men knew anything about the western herds.

When wild flowers were in bloom, prairies east of the Mississippi presented a picture now lost in farming lands. One early writer said that in June and July "these prairies seem like an ocean of flowers, of various hues, and waving to the breezes which sweep over them."

Newcomers here were amazed by the size and number of fish, just as other newcomers had been, in other parts of the continent. One fisherman mentions a black catfish, weighing 110 pounds, little dreaming that the Mississippi River "cats" were even larger. Since the first white visitors to the Middle West had come from eastern regions, this suggests that already the eastern streams were becoming a little "fished out."

Another fisherman from Boston was much startled by "a terrible fish," which he described as being "about eighteen inches long; as big as a man's wrist; with large flat head something like a bullfrog. He had four legs of the bigness of a grey squirrel's, and a tail five inches long, near two inches wide; and was of a sickly ash color, and as spiteful as the devil." The New Englander was getting his first glimpse of one of the two species of giant salamanders, still common in our eastern streams, usually known as "mud puppies," "water dogs," or "hellbenders." They swarmed in the rivers near Pittsburgh.

These salamanders are still plentiful, though most people never see them and never guess that they exist. That is because they live quietly in the ooze of river beds. Every now and then, especially in low water, they take a fisherman's bait. The appearance of the squirming, strange-looking creatures, with four unexpected legs, is just as startling now as it was to the fisherman of long ago. The animals are harmless, but most fishermen don't know that. They get frightened and cut their lines, just to get rid of the alarming little monsters.

Boone could not see all of the new country on this one hunt, lengthy though it was but he saw a great deal of it. Almost as soon as his party reached Kentucky, he set off on one of the long, solitary wilderness rambles that he loved. He went as far as Big Hill, between the Rockcastle and Kentucky Rivers, and from its summit looked out over the country, with which his name was to be associated forever.

Boone and his friends had not hunted long before there was Indian trouble. Stuart disappeared entirely. Boone found his skeleton five years later and identified it by a powder horn with his initials. A broken left arm, the bone still marked by the discoloration caused by a lead bullet, showed how he had met his end. The rest of his companions soon gave up and went home. But not Daniel Boone. By 1770, he was the only white man in all Kentucky dodging Indian hunting parties, looking for his food, laying up a store of deerskins against the day when his brother Squire would come back with fresh supplies. Enraptured, he wandered through these beautiful, primitive landscapes. A few years later, when white settlement began, he was the one white man who knew Kentucky best.

But, though Kentucky's western border is the Mississippi River, not even Daniel Boone knew much about the Father of Waters. Very likely he did not even see it, during this first year in the land for which he was to do so much. Nor did he ever attempt to explore it. That was still a task for Frenchmen.

Although it is the largest river in North America and second largest in the world, exceeded only by the Nile in length and by the Amazon in volume, and though it was one of the first American rivers seen by white men, the Mississippi was one of the last to be explored. Of all the great American rivers, only the Columbia—lying in the far Northwest, completely out of the path of early wanderers—was explored later than the Father of Waters.

Who the early explorer was that first sighted the Mississippi Delta, we do not know; but it is certain that not long after Columbus, some curious white man had been collecting information about its geography. As early as 1513, the Mississippi Delta was represented, fairly accurately, in a new edition of the ancient geography of the Greco-Egyptian astronomer, Claudius Ptolomaeus. Though it had been written more than a thousand years earlier, this old book was still being kept up to date, by the addition of new discoveries. It has been suspected that the information added in 1513 was collected, in some mysterious way, by Columbus himself. For this reason, the map is traditionally known as "the Admiral's Map." By 1520, only seven years later, Cortez sent another map, even more detailed, to the Emperor Charles V, who was also king of Spain.

Most of this information was probably based on nothing more than conversation with the Indians. But the Mississippi Delta was traced so accurately that this part of the ancient map must have been based on somebody's observation of the place itself. Who was it? No one knows. Cabeza de Vaca had sailed past the delta, but that was after 1513.

The survivors of De Soto's expedition, who sailed down the Mississipi on their way to Mexico, after their leader's death, were the first white men who had seen more of the river than the first few miles above the delta. But even they had seen only the lower four hundred miles—of which they left no real description.

After that, there was no more Spanish exploration of the Mississippi Valley for a long time. De Soto's men had gained nothing and had suffered terribly. No Spaniards wanted to explore country like that any further.

Meantime, far to the north, French explorers moving inland from the St. Lawrence, began to hear tales of a great (Missi) River (Sipi) that lay somewhere ahead. Radisson and his brother-in-law, wintering near Lake Superior in 1658, heard about the Sioux, and "a beautiful river, large, broad and deep." While La Salle was still busy with exploration in the 1670's, the French Canadian government decided that it was high time to undertake official exploration, at its own expense. About 1672 the government prepared to send Louis Jolliet to explore "the great river Mississippi, which is believed to empty in the California Sea." This official wording shows how little even the highest officials really knew about North America.

In Jolliet, they found an almost ideal man for their purpose. Born near Quebec in 1645, he had been educated at the Jesuit College there. He had given up his studies for the priesthood, had visited France, returned to Canada, and plunged into the wilderness.

As usual in expeditions of this sort, both French and Spanish, a priest was sent along to do missionary work—in this case, the famous Father Jacques Marquette, usually known simply as Père Marquette.

They were an ideal pair for the task. Marquette spoke six Indian languages. Jolliet knew the languages of the Ottawa country. Both had long experience in the wilderness. Jolliet possessed great tact and prudence. He feared nothing. Marquette was a man of singular sweetness and gentleness, utterly indifferent to worldly matters and equally incapable of fear, jealousy, or personal ambition. His temper was by nature so placid that the worst hardships of the wilderness left it wholly undisturbed.

With five companions in two bark canoes, they set forth from Mackinac Island in May of 1673. They followed the usual Indian route—from Green Bay on Lake Michigan, up the Fox River to its source, then over the low watershed (which means that it was slightly elevated ground, containing a "height of land" which drained into rivers on each side), and down the Wisconsin River into the Mississippi itself.

At Green Bay, they turned into the Fox River, helped by a gentle current, a matter of great importance to canoemen pushing upstream. The stream was full of migrating waterfowl, attracted by the wild rice, which grew so thick in those waterways that sometimes canoes had trouble getting through it. Nowadays, there is so little wild rice and the demand for it is so great, that it is all gathered before winter sets in. In those days, there was so much that a single patch might cover a space five miles by two. It was so thick that sometimes passage for a canoe had to be chopped through it.

Neither the Indians nor the waterfowl could eat enough to exhaust the endless grain supply. One small lake could produce enough to feed two thousand people. Jolliet and Marquette found the tall stalks swaying above the water, still full of grain, though it was late spring and the new growth was ready to begin.

Wilderness ways change slowly. Père Marquette described in 1673 exactly the way in which, to this very day, the Ojibway Indians of northern Minnesota and Ontario still gather their wild rice harvest. He wrote, "In the month of September, which is the proper time for this harvest, they go in canoes across these fields of wild oats, and shake the ears on their right and left into the canoes as they advance; the grain falls easily if it is ripe." Today we pay a large price for a pound of it in a few specialized grocery stores, as a perfect accompaniment to a dinner of fowl or game.

The two canoes with seven men stopped at Indian villages along their way, whose sites seemed to have been chosen with an eye to beauty. Father Marquette commented on the picturesque and beautiful views to be seen from them. As the explorers paddled silently along, they saw great numbers of moose and deer. The animals stayed near the lakes and streams in fly time as they do today, dipping into the water to escape the insects that tormented them. Today, however, these—like so many animals—have moved north, chased there by the incoming hordes of white people. In recent years, airplanes have scared them even farther northward.

There is no creature quite so grand and haughty as a great bull moose, comfortably nibbling among the lily pads of a wilderness stream. He is fearless and reluctant to move away. He seems quite as curious about people in a canoe, as they are about him. When he does throw back his mighty antlers, lifting his great nostrils haughtily and showing the fine "bell" hanging at his throat, he snorts in disdain and gives the intruder the impression of a proud proprietor, disturbed on his own land, but too well-bred a gentleman to make a fuss about it.

After more than a hundred miles of easy paddling down the Wisconsin River amid delightful scenery, Jolliet and Marquette turned into the clear water of the main current of the upper Mississippi on June 17. The river there is small compared to what it becomes farther down after the Missouri and the Ohio pour in their great floods.

As the explorers floated down the wild, silent stream between the empty lands of Iowa and Illinois, they noted the woodlands of the upper river changing to prairie country, though they never guessed at the incredible richness of the future farm lands through which they were passing. Later on, a settler said that the ground around "Kekalamazoo" in Michigan was so "fat" that it would grease your fingers! As they left Michigan and Wisconsin behind, Jolliet and Marquette were coming into country more fertile still—Iowa.

They began to notice "monstrous fish" in the Mississippi. One of these struck their canoe so violently that Marquette at first thought it was a large floating tree, knocking their canoe to pieces.

As they approached the east bank, near the spot where Alton, Illinois now stands, they beheld a startling painting on the bold cliffs, rising from the water. This was the Piasaw Bird, a mythical creature supposed to live on human flesh. Indians in the Middle West and in parts of Canada often painted pictures of this sort on rocks along the water. Some of these are in places still held sacred, even today. These paintings were unusually large and striking. They depicted two strange monsters, half beast, half bird. Père Marquette reports each painted monster was large as a calf, with horns like a deer, terrible to behold, and with red eyes. It was bearded like a tiger, the face somewhat like a man's, the body covered with scales. Its tail was so long that it swirled around the body twice, passing over the head and down between the legs, ending at last in a fish's tail. Painted in green, red, and black, these pictures were so high up on the rock, that the priest did not see how they could have been painted there at all. The strange figures were mysterious Indian "medicine."

Though the Indians had left offerings for the spirits at the monster-marked shrine in Marquette's time, something changed their feelings toward it. A hundred years later, they shot arrows at it instead. After they acquired firearms, they fired their rifles at the paintings until they were pock-marked by thousands of bullets.

On the way down-river the landscape was constantly changing. Before Jolliet and Marquette came to the site of modern St. Louis, they could hear a disturbance in the waters ahead, like the noise of a rapid. This was the violent entrance of the Missouri, or as the Indians called it, the "Pekitanoui." After "the Big Muddy" mingled with the Mississippi, the Mississippi waters were never clear again.

The Frenchmen had arrived at the time of the July floods, when the melting snows of the Rockies made their full flood force felt, hundreds of miles away. Père Marquette thought he had seen nothing more frightful than the masses of large trees, their branches tangled together till they seemed like floating islands, which came rushing out of the mouth of the "Big Muddy," toward his frail canoe. For some distance below the joining of the rivers, the explorers could see the muddy water of the Missouri along the west bank, and the clear water of the upper Mississippi, slightly tinged with green, along the east bank, the waters flowing together without mixing for sixty miles downstream. Over a hundred years later, travelers said they could drink clear water on one side of the big river, and muddy on the other.

Farther down, where the Ohio joined the Mississippi, passenger pigeons swarmed, together with wild ducks, wild geese, and wild turkeys. The travelers met occasional Indians, some of whom they visited; but when they had gone as far south as Arkansas, Père Marquette could no longer understand their language. The travelers were now far away from any of the tribes whose dialects the priest knew.

From what Indians had told them, however, Jolliet and Marquette knew that they were approaching the Gulf Coast, which was then Spanish territory. Knowing that the Spaniards wanted no white intruders, they decided to return to Canada with the notes and information they had now collected.

Turning back on July 17, they had great trouble paddling against the river's current. Near Alton, Illinois, they turned off into the Illinois River, and noted that they had never yet, in all their travels, seen anything like those wonderful, fertile prairies. Scattered on them, were thick patches of woods, wild "cattle" (buffalo), deer, wild geese, which they called "bustards," swans, ducks, beaver, and an occasional wild cat. The explorers carried their canoes overland to Lake Michigan, and in September reached Green Bay, which they had left the June before.

Jolliet went to Quebec with his journals and a map. Instead of portaging around the last rapid, he tried to shoot down it in his canoe. It overturned, and all his records of the long voyage were lost. He was almost lost himself, and was saved only after he had been in the water for several hours. He had left copies of some of his records with Père Marquette but he tried to write the story over again from memory.

The hardships of the long voyage had been too much for Père Marquette. In November of the next year he started on a mission to the Illinois Indians, but became dangerously ill on the way. When he had preached to the Illinois village, he started back for Lake Michigan. It was the beginning of winter; Père Marquette was growing weaker and weaker. When they came to the mouth of a river with a high place on the bank, Père Marquette knew his time had come, and asked to be taken ashore. He confessed the men with him, and after two or three hours he died, smiling happily, as if he saw some lovely vision above the crucifix which his sorrowing friends held out before him.

The entire course of the Mississippi, except the stretch above the Wisconsin's mouth, had now been traversed by white men. De Soto's men had traveled from Arkansas to the mouth. Marquette and Jolliet had traveled from the Wisconsin to Arkansas, and La Salle was about to explore the lower Mississippi again.

The next new land to see stretched far out across and beyond the big river—drawing wondering eyes ever westward, as the evening sun went down.

CHAPTER 16

Beyond the Mississippi

AS SOON as the eager French explorers had gained some knowledge of the Mississippi itself and had located the mouths of its great western tributaries, they began to realize that these big rivers, flowing in from the mysterious West, must open the way, through lands as yet unknown, to the far Pacific. La Salle, probably repeating what Indians had told him, believed the Missouri was navigable "for more than 1200 miles westward." This was not far wrong, for navigation in small boats. He had also learned from Indians that the country for that distance was "open and like one vast plain."

Even though there were rumors of the existence of "the Shining Mountains," it was a long time before anyone guessed just how big the Rockies really were and how hard it was going to be to get across them.

Nevertheless, as French colonies spread slowly along the Mississippi during the very early eighteenth century, passing voyageurs looked, with longer and longer thoughts, up mysterious rivers, opening off to the west. Along those streams must lie unknown lands, strange tribes, new scenes, unguessed wealth—mines such as no man knew—and ever the bright face of danger and the constant beckoning of far adventure.

Three great rivers began to seem the most promising as the Frenchmen, traveling up and down the Mississippi, began to know it better. The first, flowing into the great river about two hundred miles above its mouth, was the Red River, named from the reddish mud that colored its water. Nearly the same distance again upstream was the Arkansas. Then, almost double that distance farther north, was the Missouri, whose boiling, muddy torrent, pouring into the Mississippi, no traveler could overlook.

There were other streams, too, flowing in from the west, but these were smaller. Neither they nor the innumerable sluggish bayous, full of fish, snakes, and alligators, and overhung by the thick tunnel of overarching trees with drooping Spanish moss, seemed promising.

French attempts to explore the Far West began early. Jolliet on his homeward journey up the Mississippi in 1673 already realized that, though the Mississippi itself did not lead west, its tributaries probably did. By 1686 La Salle's faithful lieutenant, Henri Tonti, had gone some distance up the Arkansas River and built a small log fort. No one knows how far up the stream Tonti went; but by 1706 two Canadians whose names are unknown had gone west far enough to meet Spaniards coming overland from Mexico. Two years later other unidentified Frenchmen had gone up the Missouri. In 1714 and again in 1717, a young French nobleman, Louis Juchereau de St. Denis went up the Red River and then struck off, cross-country, through Texas to the Rio Grande and a Spanish mission there. The Texas countryside he found was very much like what it is today—prairie, alternating oak and pine forests, some mesquite bushes. Buffalo and other game were not in the immense quantities that roamed the prairies farther north, but St. Denis and his men found enough to live on.

St. Denis seems to have followed a route far enough south to escape the long narrow belt of tangled woodland, which later Texans were to know as "The Cross Timbers." This ran from the southern part of Kansas across what is now Oklahoma and then across Texas to within fifty or a hundred miles of the site of the modern city of San Antonio. It was a tangle of oak, hickory, elm, "shin-oak," and mats of grapevines and briars through which a man could hardly penetrate. Long after, when white settlements were growing rapidly, travelers used the Cross Timbers as a kind of base line from which to measure distances.

By 1719, though the idea of a sea passage through North America had been given up, the French frontiersman, Bénard La Harpe was suggesting that it might be possible to go west along one of the Mississippi's great tributaries and then overland to the Pacific coast. La Harpe felt sure there would be other big rivers, leading down to the Pacific, though this was long before any white man had seen the Columbia. He anticipated the great idea on which Thomas Jefferson was acting, nearly a hundred years later, when he sent Lewis and Clark up the Missouri, across the Rockies, down the Columbia, and so to the Pacific.

The Red River was the most difficult of the three western tributaries to ascend. This was not because of its current. Except for occasional rapids, it was sluggish. But navigation in pirogues (the French name for dugout canoes) was difficult because the river had two main channels and many smaller ones. It was hard to find the right one. Many channels simply opened into a lake along the banks and led the traveler nowhere.

Some of the smaller channels were so covered with overarching, mossy trees, vines, and other vegetation, that the sun could scarcely penetrate. The surface of the stream was dark even in daytime. Snakes, hanging from the branches, and alligators, swarming in the water, added to the traveler's troubles. Sometimes the river had more mud than water and canoes had to be dragged through the mud when they could not be paddled.

Near Natchitoches, the "Red River Raft" blocked the river completely. The "Raft" was an extraordinary tangle of old logs, whole trees, silt, leaves, and green vegetation. Ever changing, it was not a continuous mass. Separate "rafts" might collect for a time at bends in the river, with clear spaces between them. At times the raft was about thirty miles long. In 1805 it was reported as fifty miles long. It may, at times have choked the river for as much as a hundred miles.

Underneath this crazy mass of logs, sod and branches, gurgled the

Red River. Soil settled on the "raft," so that in some places full-sized trees grew on it. One could walk across the river on it, and in some cases horsemen are said to have ridden across without even guessing there was a river underneath them. It was 1880 before the U. S. Government was finally able to conquer it completely, after nearly fifty years of trying.

The Red River Raft has been compared to a great serpent, wriggling its way upstream as if it were a living thing. Each year the water swept new debris against its upper end. Each year the river swept logs and debris downstream from its lower end. Thus the raft crept upstream each year, choking the river and sending the water floating along the shores. It is supposed to have started about 1400 near the mouth of the river and to have writhed its way four hundred miles upstream in a little less than five hundred years.

There were similar obstructions in other western rivers in the flat delta country, but none as big as this. They were known as "floating bridges," "floating islands," or "wooden islands." These might be six to nine miles long. One was thirty feet thick. Willows ten inches in diameter grew on them.

In 1719, the Frenchman Bénard La Harpe, pushed and tugged his pirogues around the Red River Raft as best he could. Probably he had to portage a good part of the way. When he was clear of the raft, he followed a tributary, not the main stream of the Red River, northward into eastern Oklahoma. Here he found prairies with fertile black earth, game, various fruit trees, oaks, willows, and the grape vines, which in those days twined over most of North America. The Frenchmen paused to make six barrels of wine. Game included buffalo, bear, antelope, hares, rabbits, snipe, and wild turkeys. Here, as at Fort Pitt (Pittsburgh, in Pennsylvania), no one even dreamed of the rich oil deposits that lay beneath the fertile black soil. Another French expedition went up the Arkansas River that same year. It, too, failed to guess the country's wealth of oil.

News of these French expeditions soon reached the Spanish governor of Mexico. In 1720 that official sent out an expedition under Don Pedro Villasur, which also went to the Arkansas River, to see what the French were doing, then on to the middle of Nebraska.

Villasur might have brought back a fascinating description of this unknown country, but Indians almost wiped out the expedition. Only thirteen white men returned to Mexico. None of them left a description of what he had seen.

This was a bad blow to Spanish prestige among the Indian tribes. The French were quick, in the summer of 1724, to follow up the advantage and at once sent Étienne de Bourgmont through Missouri and into Kansas to promote trade. Pausing to build Fort Orleans somewhere in western Missouri, probably not far from Kansas City, he went up the Kansas River to the Paducah tribes, with whom the French were eager to form an alliance. From Fort Orleans, De Bourgmont went overland with eight white men, about a hundred Missouri Indians, and sixty-four Osages. He went up the Missouri to the mouth of the Kansas and some distance beyond, then struck south across country to the Kansas River again, up which he went till he came to the Paducah villages.

Though these Frenchmen never struck the really big buffalo herds, the travelers were agreeably amazed by the numbers they saw. In one day De Bourgmont passed thirty herds, each of four to five hundred animals. Rejoicing at the abundance of meat, they lived on buffalo tongue, without discovering the delicacy of the meat in the hump, and wasting the rest of the carcasses—each with hundreds of pounds of fresh beef.

Next, between 1739 and 1742, the brothers Paul and Pierre Mallet, with a party of eight Canadians, went up the Missouri as far as the mouth of the Platte and then overland to Santa Fé. Their explorations took them along the Canadian River from the Rockies to its mouth, and also across the states of Nebraska, Colorado, and New Mexico.

As the Mallets moved over the divide between the Platte and the Arkansas Rivers, near the headwaters of the Kansas, the country became mountainous. As they approached timbered country, they saw buffalo in herds of two and three thousand. This was probably the white man's first contact with real "buffalo country."

The immense area of country drained by the "Big Muddy" came last in the exploration of the Mississippi Valley. Soldiers of the Amer-

ican army were the men who would complete it. Before this exploration could be completed, the United States had won independence,
created a nation, and elected a third President—Thomas Jefferson.

Some time earlier, the French had acquired from the Spanish the
whole vast western country called Louisiana Territory—roughly speaking, all the land between the crest of the Rockies and the Mississippi
River. This is the immense territory President Jefferson bought from
the Emperor Napoleon. The President did not know what he had
bought. Neither did the Emperor. Two American army officers went
out to see. It was their expedition which found, at last, a northwestern
route to the Pacific—though it was not the salt water "Northwest
Passage" explorers had sought so long.

These partners in discovery were Meriwether Lewis and William
Clark.

CHAPTER 17

Lewis and Clark Go
Up the Missouri

IN THE three hundred years that had passed between the coming of Columbus and the early 1800's, the picture of the New World in men's minds had naturally changed enormously. The idea of a water passage through North America vanished.

Starting along the eastern seaboard, white settlements had swiftly spread, with the arrival of more and ever more people from Europe, until they were flourishing as far west as the banks of the Mississippi. St. Louis was already a civilized little town. There were a few settlements, up the Missouri River, west of it. There were also Spanish settlements in distant California, and ships were putting in to trade with the Indians in Oregon and along the Pacific coast of Canada.

As early as 1720, a Jesuit, instructed to examine future land routes to the Pacific, had suggested two possibilities: One was to establish a series of trading posts among the Sioux, as bases for an overland journey. The other was to ascend the Missouri River and then go on, by routes which at that time could only be guessed at, to the Pacific coast. The first scheme was impossible. The Jesuit father had not known what the Sioux Indians were like, though the French soon found out. The Missouri route, on the other hand, was promising.

Later during the 1700's, as we have seen, explorers examined other streams leading west from the Mississippi only to find that they did not open the way to reach the Western Sea. The Missouri River route was still the most promising.

As the turn of the century approached, the rhythm of westward exploration quickened. The trader, Jacques d'Eglise lived among the Missouri Indians from 1790 to 1792 and is the first who left even a meager record of what he saw there. Eglise was soon followed by another trader, Jean Baptiste Trudeau, who in 1794-95 went as far as the Arikara villages, near the boundary between North and South Dakota. Other traders ventured some distance into the Dakotas, and a few Canadians came overland into Mandan country, which Vérendrye had visited long before.

The first real account of the country, however, comes from the Canadian trader, Pierre Antoine Tabeau, who went up the Missouri in 1802 with Régis Loisel and remained among the Indians for several years. He was already there to greet Lewis and Clark, who knew all about him and were looking for him, when they reached the Arikara villages near the northern boundary of South Dakota. Tabeau's journal survives in two copies, one in the Library of Congress, the other at Yale. A third has been lost.

But it remained for the Virginians, Lewis and Clark, to make the first complete report of the Missouri Country. William Clark was a former Regular Army officer, used to wilderness life, who had had experience making maps and in what we should now call military intelligence. He was skillful enough with pen and pencil to make sketches of birds and plants, though landscapes were beyond his artistic power. Meriwether Lewis had been given special scientific training for the expedition. Both these officers and several of the enlisted personnel kept diaries. Through their writings and drawings, we know more about the earliest days on the Missouri than we know about any other part of the ever-advancing first frontier.

When Lewis and Clark started up the Missouri, in May of 1804, pioneer days in the new American territory of Louisiana were approaching their end. Daniel Boone and others had brought in American settlers, some years before the new United States acquired Louisiana from France for the small sum of fifteen million dollars. Settlements now stretched up the river to St. Charles, Femme Osage, and beyond. Northwest to a point beyond Bismarck, North Dakota, a few adventurous whites had penetrated, to hunt, trap, or trade.

From the Pacific coast eastward, one or two inquisitive sailors had taken small boats up the Columbia River for about a hundred miles. On the Canadian side, Alexander Mackenzie had crossed the continent in 1793. Spanish settlements in California had reached a respectable age.

But between the thin fringe of half-explored or partly settled territory on the Pacific and the frontier advancing from the Mississippi was a wide unknown—represented on all maps then and for years afterward, as an empty white space. Through this Lewis and Clark, with what they proudly named their "Corps of Discovery," made their way. Past lands that later would be Missouri, Kansas, Iowa, Nebraska, and the two Dakotas, they waded, splashed, paddled, poled, and "cordelled" their way, until, in Montana, they left the plains behind them and approached the Rockies. (Where the current was too strong to paddle against, and the water too deep to wade while pushing the loaded boats, men walking along the bank, pulled the boats by ropes. This was called cordelling.) They had thus crossed the various terrain compartments known to geographers as the Mississippi flood plains, the high plains, and the Missouri Plateau—which is not in Missouri at all, but in Montana and the Dakotas. Almost imperceptibly, the land had risen under them, so that when they left their boats at last they were only a short distance from the Continental Divide, though they had to climb much higher before they could find a pass that would take them through the Rockies.

Lewis and Clark, and the men with them, saw thousands of miles of unknown, unspoiled, untouched, primitive country, lying as it had lain for ages, and as varied as it was wild. They watched it change as they struggled slowly up the Missouri toward the Rockies.

Often the scenery had romantic beauty. From the rich prairie and timber lands, they passed up the Missouri until many kinds of trees disappeared, and there was little left but willow and dwarf cotton-wood.

The expedition's chief difficulties at first were snags and collapsing banks. Snags were a Missouri River specialty. For hundreds of miles the Missouri flowed between huge bluffs, at first of stone, then almost wholly of thick clay. When the mighty stream was in spring flood it gnawed beneath the bluffs, carrying away single trees and sometimes whole woodlands at once. Dragged along the bottom, banged by floating timber, scoured by sand, the water-logged tree trunks embedded their heavy roots in the bottom while the jagged stumps of broken limbs thrust up through the water or lurked just under its surface ready to rip through any river boat that happened to strike them.

Sometimes they swayed up and down at intervals of several minutes, rising suddenly under the bow of a boat where an instant before the smooth surface had seemed perfectly safe. Sharp stubs would rise in the water with enough violence to smash through the bottom of any river craft. Rivermen soon learned to load their pirogues heavily at the stern and lightly at the bow, so that they could ride up on the snags easily, without too much damage. Clark had to stop the whole expedition soon after it started, in order to reload each boat in this way.

Making camp for the night on the Missouri's banks, boatmen were sometimes appalled to find the ground giving way beneath them, while big trees that edged the banks crashed down around them. The sandbank under a Lewis and Clark camp once crumbled at half past one in the morning, while everyone but the guard was sound asleep. Wakened by the sentry, they jumped for the boats, loaded them, and got away just as the bank under which their boats had been moored caved in completely.

The lower Missouri was edged by really big trees—cottonwoods, several feet through, with trunks rising seventy or eighty feet before the branches began. Sometimes, as one of these giants fell, its roots remained embedded in the bank. It then became a kind of dam, catching all the debris that the river constantly swept down, floating logs, moving snags (called "sawyers"), and dead buffalo, whose carcasses sometimes floated as far as St. Louis. There were other obstructions such as the Red River Raft, but on a smaller scale, since the Missouri's current was too swift to allow anything like the Raft's miles of tangled timber to accumulate. But they were bad enough, especially when the swift current rushing past the end of the embarras, which was the name for these obstructions, made it impossible to go around it, and the boatmen had to cut a way through, while trying to hold their boats steady. Often this had to be done in the summer's heat which compelled the crews to work with their shirts off, while mosquitoes bit till the men were "covered with blood and swellings." Horseflies and gadflies were even worse than mosquitoes.

Settlement had already made some kinds of game scarce along the lower Missouri. By this time there were no longer any buffalo; the really big herds roamed far up the river, in the Dakotas and Montana. Preying on them was that terror of the plains, the grizzly bear, about which white men still knew practically nothing.

But there was still plenty of game for the hunters of the expedition, hunting along the banks of the river, to kill "for the pot." Wild geese, ducks and wild turkeys were common, and there were still many deer. Not all the wildlife had been driven away. The sandhill cranes, now almost gone, then haunted both Mississippi and Missouri, sometimes flying so high that they could not be seen, though their harsh, grating cries still came down through the air.

Lewis and Clark just missed being caught by a prairie fire on the Missouri, which swept past their camp, burning two Indians and injuring others. When the rushes that grew along the riverbanks dried out, they were like kindling. Fires spread so fast that a man on foot had no hope of escaping alive, unless he could get out on the river.

In the autumn, immense numbers of migrating squirrels crowded into the Missouri River, just as they did in some rivers of the East. Nothing stopped them. In thick columns they rushed excitedly forward to some unknown goal, no matter what lay in their path. Even so wide a river as the Missouri did not stop them. They drowned by thousands. Some suffocated in the mud along the banks and their bodies were pushed down until they made a bridge for others pressing on behind them.

The animal life of the plains changed as the Corps of Discovery crossed the line that is now the southern border of South Dakota. Here they killed their first buffalo—a day's supply of meat for the entire expedition of a little over a hundred men.

The buffalo herds increased in size as Lewis and Clark ascended the river. Having no idea as yet how big a herd could be, the men were at first surprised to see a herd of about five hundred animals, which they thought "great numbers." In real buffalo country, a single herd might extend for twenty-five miles. In a short time to come, experienced hunters were to declare that when the weather was right, they could detect a big buffalo herd out of sight over the horizon, simply by the cloud of vapor which rose as the animals breathed. (A young lieutenant who once sat with Benteen, the hero of the Custer massacre, on a high hill giving a view of twenty miles in all directions, reported that Benteen assured him that there were three hundred thousand buffalo to be seen below them "in one view.")

As the great herds appeared, Lewis and Clark also began to see other animals typical of the new region they were entering. The first prairie dog town, a small one of only four acres, created much excitement, though it was not so remarkable as it seemed. Some prairie dog towns covered a hundred acres.

The Americans now saw for the first time the brilliant black and white western magpie, unknown in the East, which they thought a beautiful bird. They captured four, tended them in cages all winter, and sent them back to President Jefferson, who was fond of birds and habitually kept a tame mockingbird hopping about the White House.

On the prairie, which looked smooth and grassy, "like a bowling green," the explorers from their boats could watch buffalo, deer, elk, antelope, bear, turkeys, and ducks, all feeding at once. Wild pigeons fluttered about in enormous numbers, especially where small oak trees provided acorn mast.

At the Mandan Indian villages beyond Bismarck, North Dakota, the Lewis and Clark expedition went into camp for the winter. They built a strong fort and maintained an alert sentinel, day and night, so that, in spite of threats from the Sioux, they were never attacked.

In the spring of 1805, the captains sent one boat down the Missouri, back to civilization. It carried some men whom they did not want to take any farther. With them they sent magpies and prairie dogs to President Jefferson, who was always interested in new animals. Only a few white men had ever gone beyond the Mandan Villages, and they had not gone very far. From the Mandan country, the rest of the Lewis and Clark Expedition was taking its plunge into wholly unknown lands.

Across Montana they went. Beaver began to appear more frequently as they approached the Rockies, such fine ones that Lewis thought their pelts the best by far that he had ever seen.

"Coal"—actually lignite—could sometimes be seen along the river. One bed was on fire, burning with a "strong sulphurious smell." Alkali began to appear in white patches on hills, riverbanks and sandbars. The river dissolved enough of it to make the water unpleasant to drink. On one occasion it poisoned Lewis.

All winter long, Lewis and Clark's Americans had been listening skeptically to Indian stories of grizzly bears. The Mandans said that sometimes they could kill a grizzly, but more often the grizzlies killed them. A grizzly hunt was as dangerous as war, they said. A necklace of the bear's great claws was one of the highest distinctions a warrior could achieve. But the Americans were not much impressed. No doubt grizzlies were hard for Indians to kill with lances, bows, arrows, but it would be a different story when the bears faced the U. S. Army rifles of the Corps of Discovery.

They had not gone very far beyond the Mandan villages when they began to see bear tracks along the river, especially where there were dead buffalo. The footprints were larger than any these experienced hunters had ever seen. They measured one. It was eleven inches long and seven and a half inches across. Though tracks now appeared constantly, the bears themselves never showed up. Lewis noted in his journal that they must be very wary and shy. The whole expedition was now "anxious to meet with some of these bears."

They got their wish, soon enough. Within a few days, Lewis himself, accompanied by one soldier, ran into two grizzlies. Both men foolishly fired at the same time. This overconfidence left them helpless, with both rifles empty. If the two bears had attacked together, the two men would have been mauled to death then and there. Luckily, only one of the animals attacked. The other fled. Lewis fled, too--a distance of some eighty yards. The badly wounded bear gave up and let Lewis get away, and began a series of short, swift rushes. All this was very dangerous, for up to a hundred yards a grizzly, big as he is, can move as fast as a horse. The two hunters ran about, trying to keep away from the bear till they could pour some powder into their rifles and ram home their bullets. They finally managed to reload, fired again, and killed the beast—after which they made the humiliating discovery that this was just a half-grown cub.

Although grizzlies could be eaten, they were not so palatable as the black bear. They tasted like "coarse pork." The oil, however, was valuable in cooking, better than lard. Bear fat soon came to be preferred to butter or lard in New Orleans, and hunters learned to boil it "upon sweet-bay leaves" which improved its keeping qualities. It kept sweet and good in any season. One big bear when fat in the fall, in preparation for his winter's sleep, might provide thirty gallons of bear oil.

The trouble was that grizzlies were almost unkillable or, as Lewis put it, "hard to die." The muzzle-loading rifles of the early nineteenth century did not have the velocity, and hence the shocking-power, of modern express rifles. Sometimes, even with a shot in the heart the great animals ran a quarter of a mile. The one really vital spot, the brain, was protected by a thick covering of flesh and a thick frontal bone. Only twice did the Lewis and Clark expedition ever bring down a grizzly at a single shot. The interpreter, Drouillard, a professional woodsman and hunter taken along specially for his skill, did it once, and Clark, an expert infantryman, was the other to accomplish the feat. The Lewis and Clark party had some narrow escapes from the grizzlies, but no one was ever actually hurt.

By the time they were nearing Great Falls, in Montana, it was the end of summer. As autumn drew on, the mating season of the buffalo began. All over the plains, huge bulls were locked in battles to the death, amid deafening bellows. Clark once complained in his journal that the noise kept him from sleeping. Lewis described a scene near Great Falls where the buffalo bulls kept up such a tremendous roaring that they could be heard miles away. There were so many of them that the roar was continuous. Lewis thought that, at one place on the river, he saw ten thousand buffalo at once, crowded into a two-mile circle.

Always a nature lover, Lewis often left the boats to roam the banks, while the men brought the heavily loaded craft upstream. On one of these rambles, with one companion, he was the first to reach Great Falls, a magnificent spectacle no white man had ever seen. The country had become more "rolling," after the expedition left the broad flat plains. From higher ground it was possible to see over vast territory and Lewis now saw "infinitely more" buffalo than he had ever "witnessed at a view."

Sending several men out to kill some beef, he pushed on until his ears were "saluted with the agreeable sound of a fall of water," and presently he could see the spray arise above the plain like a column of smoke. Hurrying down the little hill on which he stood, he beheld the "sublimely grand spectacle" of the Falls of the Missouri, which is still impressive even though a power dam has somewhat tamed its primitive grandeur. Much moved by the spectacle, Lewis wrote a long description and wished that he could paint in order to give the world some idea of this truly magnificent and "sublimely grand object, which has from the commencement of time been concealed from the view of civilized man."

The enlisted man with Lewis was not in the least enraptured. He was more interested in reflecting that there are always more fish below falls. Presently he produced a large number of trout, sixteen to twenty-three inches in length, for supper.

In spite of the immense food supplies that game provided here, there were no Indians. In five months of travel over the long stretch from near Bismarck, North Dakota, to the foothills of the Rockies, the expedition had not seen a single human being. There was not even much "Indian sign." A moccasin, a kind of football, some old lodge poles, and a few similar traces, were all they found to show they were not the only representatives of mankind who had ever passed that way.

At last, as they approached the western edge of Montana, they began to see great smokes on the prairie. Though they did not know it, these were the signals of a Shoshone band, calling in their few scattered hunters from the buffalo plains. The explorers also found a spot where an Indian had silently watched their camp from a hillock and as silently departed.

Animal life on the plains began to change again. They were amazed at "a large herd of Bighorned animals"—Rocky Mountain goats—which they saw moving easily about on almost perpendicular rocky cliffs.

All around them, various wild berry bushes were coming into fruit. Even here, North America was a land of small fruits—as was thankfully noted by all early visitors. The bears liked all the berries, and ate them impartially.

Presently the river brought the Americans to the "Gates of the Mountains," the most remarkable cliffs they had ever seen, which are still called by the name the explorers gave them, and are still one of North America's most magnificent bits of scenery, though temporarily marred by forest fires. Rising to a height of 1,200 feet, sheer from the water's edge, the perpendicular cliffs with their projecting rocks seemed ready to crash down on the boats. The whole river, compressed here to a mere 150 yards in width, was deep and swift.

Beyond this, the Missouri broke into its "Three Forks," to which Lewis and Clark gave the names they still bear—the Madison, Gallatin, and Jefferson rivers. Though the expedition was now in the very heart of the Montana gold-mining country, nobody noticed the shining specks that lay in the clear, cold water under their keels. They were too intent on pushing forward. The stream was getting swifter, narrower, colder. The Great Continental Divide lay just ahead. The early Montana winter was coming. Originally, they had expected to finish their exploration and be back in St. Louis in one year. Already a year and a half had passed and they were still going west to the Pacific. The second winter was upon them.

The expedition was now in great danger—not from Indians but from the absence of Indians. The white men could not go much farther with their boats. It was too late in the season to turn back—the river would soon be frozen behind them. Game here was scarce. It would be almost impossible to get food if the little band now tried to "fort up" for the winter, as they had done successfully the year before amid the plenty of the Dakota prairies and with the company of the Mandan Indians.

Though it was only September, the weather was already getting chill. In a few more weeks heavy snowstorms would block the Rocky Mountain passes. The only hope was to carry out their original plan, however impossible it now began to seem. They must get horses from friendly Indians and make a dash across the Rockies before the early winter of the mountainous highlands set in. But where were the Indians?

During several discouraging days while they sought for Indians— Indians with horses—they found one cause for hope. Sacagawea, the young Indian wife of their French-Canadian interpreter, Toussaint Charbonneau, had begun to recognize bits of familiar scenery from her childhood days. She was a Shoshone, who as a little girl, had been captured and taken to the Minnetaree country. Lewis and Clark had found Sacagawea and her husband, living among the Mandans the winter before. Knowing they would need interpreters, they had taken the couple and their baby along, when they started west in the spring. They were now in Shoshone country. Sacagawea's knowledge of the language was their only hope. At last Lewis succeeded in making contact with a band of Shoshones which—by what seems at first thought a miraculous coincidence—had as their chief, Ca-me-âh-wait, Sacagawea's brother and was the very band from which she had been kidnapped.

Deeply moved, brother and sister recognized each other. The real-life drama of this moment impressed the tough soldiers of the expedition. But the coincidence was not so great as it seemed. The river route the expedition had been following was the natural passage east and west. Naturally it led them straight to Sacagawea's native country, where, just as naturally, they met her kin.

With horses supplied by the Shoshones, the expedition hurried on. Over the Continental Divide, through the Lemhi Pass, across the Bitterroot Mountains, down the Bitterroot River they went—almost to Missoula, Montana—and then up and over the terrible Lolo Trail.

Horses slipped and fell. Snow turned to rain and sleet. Animals almost disappeared, and the few goats, deer, pheasants, and ducks they saw were hard to shoot.

Up the Lolo Trail they climbed, through high mountain country, covered with eight different kinds of pine, spruce, tamarack, and fir trees, many of which had fallen either from wind or fire. The side of one mountain had been burned off completely. The footing was desperate. Horses fell repeatedly. One rolled a full hundred yards. Animal life at such heights was scarce; and, though they saw a few deer, they killed none and had to eat one after another of their precious pack animals. Rocks and endless fallen timber obstructed their way and the cold gradually dampened the spirits of the party.

Knowing that nothing is quite so good for morale as food, Clark hurried forward with a small hunting party, hoping to send back meat. He failed, but suddenly, "from the top of a high part of the Mountain" (probably the modern Rocky Ridge) he found himself looking down into the vast Clearwater Valley in Idaho. Delighted with this gracious view of an immense plain and level country after their desperate mountain crossing, Clark's group camped that night without anything to eat. Their reward came the next day when they entered the beautiful wooded valley of the Clearwater. The river ran so swiftly, for all its smoothness, that it made a curious hissing sound as it flowed.

Lewis's men, following after him, had eaten a last meal in the mountains that was a mixture of pheasant, wolf meat, horse meat, and crawfish gathered from a brook, "not knowing where the next was to be found." The whole party now made a long halt to recover from the mountain crossing. Some of the men were so exhausted that they could not quite finish the march and lay by the way, till horses could be sent back for them. Lewis himself was barely able to ride a gentle horse. Game was still scarce. They bought food from Indians, but their diet of roots and dried salmon made everybody ill.

However, they had at last explored the entire length of the Missouri —something no man, white or Indian, had ever done—and they had crossed the Rockies. The rest of their adventure is part of the story of the Columbia River and the Pacific Coast. After they paused to recuperate, they started off enthusiastically down the Clearwater to make some more history.

CHAPTER 18

"The Coast"

THE FIRST white explorer to set foot on California soil was probably Ferdinand de Alarcón. There is a story that a Chinese explorer visited the California coast near Monterey, about the time Hannibal was attacking Rome (217 B.C.). The Chinese rover is even said to have praised the California climate, as all Californians of the twentieth century love to do. There is also a story that still another Chinese expedition was somewhere along the Pacific coast about the fifth century A.D.

But these are doubtful tales about the exploits of shadowy figures in ancient Oriental history, unconfirmed, perhaps wholly misunderstood. Possibly these things, or something like them, may have happened. There is no way now of being sure.

There is no doubt that Alarcón had a good claim to being the first white man in California, though even with Alarcón one cannot be quite positive. Alarcón was the hopeful Spanish naval commander who tried to support Coronado's expedition overland, to Kansas—by sailing up the Gulf of Califorina and into the mouth of the Colorado

River! He certainly saw California soil. But he failed to say on which side of the Colorado he went ashore. As a result, we do not know whether he set foot on the California side of the river, or the Arizona side. It does not matter very much. His journey led to nothing, and he left little description of what he found.

Even if Alarcón really was the first white man to land in California, he was not the first white man to see it. On September 28, 1539, Francisco de Ulloa, another sailor from Mexico, had looked across from the Gulf of Califorina and—far in the distance—had seen many mountaintops. Those shimmering peaks were certainly in what Spaniards would soon be calling "Alta California." De Ulloa did no real exploring. He came, took one quick look, and sailed away.

The first real exploration about which one can be sure, was by a Portuguese sea captain in the Spanish service, Juan Rodríguez Cabrillo, sent out by the Mexican government in 1542. With two small ships, a priest, such sailors as would join the risky enterprise, eight months' supply of food, and Indian interpreters, he sailed on June 27.

Of Cabrillo himself nothing is known, save that he had been both soldier and sailor for the Spanish king, a conquistador in Mexico, who was regarded by his superiors as "a good man and well versed in navigation"—as, indeed, his exploits proved.

Cabrillo sailed up the coast of Lower California, passing the place where the southern boundary of the United States would one day be, and reached San Diego at the end of September, 1542. Probably he arrived on September 29, for he piously named the new harbor for San Miguel, whose day it is. From San Diego, he went to Santa Catalina and then to San Pedro Bay, which must have been thickly populated by Indians, since he named it Bahía de los Fumos, because he saw the smoke of many campfires. Crossing Santa Monica Bay, he found another Indian town, probably near Point Mugu. He anchored near a beautiful valley, from which he could see high, broken mountaintops. Here he learned from the Indians of a river which never reached the sea. This was probably the Santa Clara, which is believed, at that time, to have ended in a bog.

Thence Cabrillo went on up the coast to a point somewhere near Dos Pueblos Canyon, and met what must have been the Chumash Indians, friendly, dressed only in skins, and well supplied with food. In their lank black hair they wore many flint, bone, and wooden daggers, many of which have since been dug up by modern archeologists. Cabrillo was surprised to find them living in houses with gable roofs.

Apparently Cabrillo went as far north as the Oregon coast. Like all later coastal explorers for two hundred years, he failed to see San Francisco Bay but, on the return journey, he put in at Monterey Bay. For two days in November, 1540, Cabrillo sailed about the bay looking for a harbor, but was afraid to go ashore because of the surf.

Soon after this, Cabrillo was injured in a fall, from the effects of which he died in January, 1543. His pilot, Bartolomé Ferrer, taking over command, resolutely turned north again. Sailing to what may have been the Oregon coast, he found evidence that a large river was somewhere near, which must have been the Columbia. Without trying to enter and explore the river itself, he finally brought his ships safely home to Mexico.

Ferrer was much impressed by the stretch of coast between Point Carmel and Cape St. Martin. Here, he said, "The land is very high. There are mountains which seem to reach the heavens, and the sea beats on them; sailing close to land, it appears as though they would fall on the ships."

There was not much in Ferrer's report, however, to inspire the Mexican government with further immediate interest in the Pacific coast. Plainly there was nothing in those wild parts remotely resembling the Aztec or Inca empires; and the gold-hungry Spaniards never guessed that they had been sailing past one of the greatest gold fields of all time. Not until 1570 did they again concern themselves with Alta California. Even then, they did no exploring but merely listened with alarm to wild rumors that the English explorers had found the long-sought Northwest Passage, or Strait of Anian, and were raiding from the north, looting Mexico and Peru.

There is no evidence that anyone else visited California and Oregon —certainly no one left a record—until, in 1579, Francis Drake (not yet a knight) came sailing north over the Pacific. He had left Plymouth, England, in 1577, crossed the Atlantic, passed through the Straits of Magellan "with its hell-dark nights and the merciless fury of tempestuous storms," and then had sailed north along the South American and Mexican coasts, raiding as he went. His arrival was a painful surprise to the Spaniards who, supposing themselves completely secure in a Pacific that was all their own, had taken no defensive precautions whatever. Off Peru, the astounded crew of an unarmed treasure galleon watched with disgust, while Drake transferred to his own ships their collection of jewels and precious stones, thirteen or fourteen chests full of coin, eighty pounds of gold, and twenty-six tons of silver. (In the end, Drake took home to England plunder worth four million dollars.)

After Drake had stripped the galleon, he realized there was no use trying to capture any more treasure. With his ships loaded to the gunwales, he turned northward to carry out—or at least to pretend to carry out—one of his missions, which was to search for the Strait of Anian. The Strait of Anian did not exist, and Drake rather doubted its existence; still, he had been told to look for it.

Therefore he sailed north, nearly to the present American-Canadian border and, on June 5, 1579, was driven by heavy weather into what was perhaps Chetko Bay, Oregon, almost exactly at 42°. Then back, through "thick stinking fogs, which nothing but the wind could remove," he came south. Just north of San Francisco, he found the land all low plains, with some few hills covered with snow, and then for fourteen days they could not see the sun for fog.

If Drake had run on down the coast, he would have found the Golden Gate and San Francisco Bay; but just around Point Reyes, he spied white cliffs like those of Dover—at home in England—and a conveniently hard beach.

As the *Golden Hind*'s bottom needed cleaning and repair, he careened her on the beach. While the ship's carpenters were at work, the Englishmen went a little way inland, though not far enough to discover San Francisco Bay, only about thirty miles to the south. They were surprised to find the whole country infested with a strange little animal that burrowed in the earth. These were the California gophers, or ground squirrels, which swarmed all over the state until modern times, when their inconveniently large numbers were reduced deliberately.

Because the white banks and cliffs reminded the sailors of the white cliffs of their homeland, they named the country New Albion—Albion being an old poetical name for Great Britain. Otherwise the California coast did not make a very good impression. In his book of travels, *The World Encompass'd,* Drake said the region looked "unhandsome and deformed" showing treees without leaves, and the ground without greenness in those months of June and July when he was there. He had arrived in the middle of a dry summer, when the brown California landscape was very different from the moist green English countryside. But when they went a little way inland from the coast, the Englishmen found it to be much better than the shore, and Drake reported here "a goodly country, with fruitful soil, stored with many blessings fit for the use of man."

Before he departed, Drake took formal possession of the country, in the name of Queen Elizabeth. He had brought along a brass plate, probably for this very purpose. This was engraved with Her Majesty's name and her claim to the country. He added the queen's picture and the royal coat of arms by fastening a silver sixpence—which, of course, had both on it—in a hole cut in the brass. Having completed this formal taking possession of the new lands, Drake sailed away for the Farrallones Islands, where he took aboard a supply of seal meat and sea birds, and then voyaged on across the Pacific, to the Orient. Tradition among the Indians has it that he left some pigs ashore, which multiplied rapidly and greatly astonished later Spanish explorers.

Indians were soon pounding at his plate with stone axes; and there is not much doubt that the sixpence was picked out for the adornment of some warrior. The post rotted away and the brass plate fell to the ground. Then, one day in 1923, a San Francisco banker went fishing on the Laguna River, near Drake's Bay. While the banker fished, his chauffeur, idling about, found a dull, flat, dirty piece of metal, five by eight inches and about an eighth of an inch thick. It seemed to have lettering and the chauffeur, having nothing else to do, was curious enough to wash it off. But as he still could not read it and as his employer was not in the least interested, he tossed it in the car and left it. Sometime later, tired of carrying it around, he threw it down by the roadside between San Quentin and Kentfield. Here someone else must have found it, carried it a while, then thrown it away again; for when next found, the plate was some distance away.

In 1926, a resident of Oakland, picnicking near the head of San Quentin Bay, found Drake's brass plate once again; decided it was just the thing to use in repairing his automobile; put it away. Some months later, getting the plate out for use, he became curious as he noted markings on it. By great good luck, he showed it to a pupil of Professor H. E. Bolton, of the University of California, who had long been advising his students to keep a sharp eye out for Drake's plate, which he had long hoped would turn up.

The question now was authenticity, American historians having learned from experience not to take "finds" of this sort at their face value. Practical jokers have for years been "planting" forged inscriptions both on stone and metal. Since the plate, if genuine, would be one of the treasures of the University of California, it was decided that the tests to prove authenticity had better be made in laboratories elsewhere. The plate was submitted to Dr. Colin Fink, a Columbia University electrochemist.

Under tests of every conceivable sort, the old plate "stood up" successfully. Metallurgical tests showed that the metal was an Elizabethan alloy, not a modern one, containing more magnesium than modern brass. It had been hammered in the ancient way, not rolled in a modern foundry. Its three-hundred-year-old patina was natural, just such as might, chemically speaking, have been expected from the soil in which it was found—and which was also tested. A fragment of plant tissue, caught in a crevice, had been there long enough to be mineralized.

Only certain indentations, made after the letters had been cut, were puzzling. Then someone had an idea. The technicians borrowed a prehistoric stone axe from an archeologist, whacked at another plate of brass—and got the same sort of markings. After that, there was no more question. This was Drake's plate. Today it is proudly exhibited in the library at Berkeley.

Drake's raid in the Pacific startled the Spaniards, but not enough to make them do anything about settlements in California, where he had landed. A new report came a few years later, however, in 1584,

when a Spanish naval officer, Francisco de Gali, commanding the
Manila galleon, which brought porcelain and silk from the Orient to
Mexico every year, took a more northerly course than usual. Sailing
south along the California coast, he noticed "a very high and fair
land with many trees, wholly without snow." He also noticed the
great numbers of seals. Since Gali had a high reputation, this stirred
up some interest among Spanish officials and the captain was asked
to advise them as to possible permanent settlement in California. Nothing was done, however.

Three years later came the English raider, Thomas Cavendish, who
appeared in the Pacific unexpectedly and captured a galleon loaded
with silk and gold. The worried Spaniards began to think about a
port of refuge for their ships, somewhere along the newly discovered
coast. If any more English appeared, their galleons were going to
need it. Two other mariners, running along the coast as far as 39°
and perhaps even 41°, brought in reports of fisheries, timber, fragrant
plants—a rich land.

On board the galleon Cavendish had captured, there had been an
adventurous businessman from Mexico, named Sebastián Vizcaíno.
He lost a fortune when the English seized the ship's cargo. He could
not help realizing that a protected Spanish port in California might
prevent such raids. Several times during the next fifteen years, he
went "on a discovery" to California or Lower California. It was his
party which, in 1602, first noted "a large shell fish with conques equal
to the finest mother of pearl"—in other words, the abalone, now much
prized by Californians. It would, however, be some centuries before
hungry Californians would discover that the creature was just as valuable for "abalone steaks," as for its beautiful shells. As every one else
had done, thus far, Vizcaíno failed to notice the immense expanse of
San Francisco Bay, not easily seen from the sea.

In spite of all this small-scale exploration, it was not until the
second half of the eighteenth century that the Spaniards began serious
land exploration in California, with a view to permanent occupation.
By that time, the Spanish government knew it had to do something.
There were rumors that Russians were commencing to push danger-

ously far south, from Alaska. Then, too, the English still claimed "New Albion."

In 1769, an enterprising Spanish official named Gaspar de Portolá took command of three separate exploring parties, which set out from Mexico, one by sea and two by land. Portolá was to be the governor of the new Spanish province of California. He hoped that his three separate parties would all make their way safely to what is now San Diego. His soldiers were then to set up garrisons at San Diego and Monterey, while the priests established missions under the general direction of Father Serra. Thanks to several diaries, we know a good deal about what these first land adventurers saw in primitive California.

The country around San Diego harbor was "a large level place in the midst of great meadows and plains." There were so few trees that firewood had to be brought mostly from the mountains. The San Diego River, however, had banks covered with willows, alders, poplars, and cottonwoods. It was overgrown, like the rest of the country, with "very fragrant roses," while the eternal grapevines covered the plains.

Like most of the California rivers, the San Diego was a dream of beauty. The Sacramento was "like a park." Only the San Joaquin was miry and without trees.

Few Indians were to be seen, but well-trodden paths showed their presence, as earlier sea explorers had noted in hasty trips ashore.

California meadows, such as these first adventurers saw, have now been much changed by the introduction of cattle, which wiped out many of the native bunch grasses, and later by overgrazing, produced much erosion. After Spanish settlement began, such European weeds as black mustard, wild oat, and filaree, began to take over the landscape of the coastal hills. Later still, the '49-ers and the introduction of hydraulic mining turned streams from their beds, piled up mounds of stone where mining operations required, and created ugly scars on the landscape. Only now, in our own twentieth century has Nature at last smoothed over most of the damage they did. Sheep grazing later disfigured the flowered and beautiful mountain meadows, but even here Nature has repaired the ravages of man. Lumbering destroyed many of the groves of redwoods, but many of them still rise into the sky, proudly as of old.

As soon as the whole force had assembled at San Diego, Portolá led a small group to find Monterey. Following the coast as far as modern Los Angeles, they went up the San Fernando Valley, back to the sea again, down the Santa Clara Valley, north along the coast, then a little way inland to San Luis Obispo, once more to the sea, along the coast, over the Sierra Santa Lucia down the Salinas Valley, and again along the coast to the vicinity of San Francisco.

Their journey lay through rich and unknown country. There were herds of antelope and many rabbits. Flocks of migrant wild geese and ducks were settling down for the winter, to enjoy the mild climate. San Jacinto Lake, as Portolá saw it, was "as full of white geese as water," though today both geese and lake have vanished from the San Jacinto Valley.

The going was hard but it was not really a dangerous adventure, especially since the Indians were not hostile. The country itself made the main difficulty for the explorers. Though trails ran in every direction, they were at best mere footpaths, which no horse had ever trodden—there had never been a horse in California before. An advance party of Spaniards and Indians had to ply spades, picks, axes, and crowbars to get a way open for the pack train. The horses were nervous at every strange sight and smell. A coyote, fox, bird, or even a whirl of dust was enough to set them stampeding through the woods, falling over precipices, laming or otherwise injuring themselves. The travelers killed some antelope and bears, heard mountain lions, were disturbed by earthquakes (on one occasion, nine in five days), and were shocked to find some of the Indians totally unclothed. But roses were with them all the way, and there were other shrubs they did not know. The friendly coastal Indians here practiced no agriculture. Why trouble? Nature gave them all they needed.

One priest mentioned a fragrance which came and went several times, especially on the way between San Luis Obispo and Monterey. The odor was sometimes very strong, then barely perceptible, then vanishing altogether, with no air stirring. He dismounted repeatedly to smell the wild flowers. They were fragrant too, but never so sweet as the mysterious, unexplained odor which, he thought, was either ambergris washed up along the coast, or "some sweet vapor which the land gives forth."

The Spaniards saw many bears and bear tracks all the way along the route from San Diego northward. Sometimes the creatures had torn the earth, leaving it "plowed up and full of holes which they make in searching for the roots they live on."

San Francisco Bay, which everyone had missed for more than two-hundred years, was discovered at last—quite by accident. A party of soldiers, chasing a deer, reached the crest over which the animal had disappeared and came suddenly upon a great inland sea at their feet, blue waters stretching away into hills which sheltered distant bays, the extent of which they could only guess at. The soldiers left no description of the future site of San Francisco at the moment when the white man came, but their superiors did:

"The land surrounding this immense base offers, when seen from the sea, a very pleasing view. For, looking south, one sees the Sierra de Santa Lucia, sending out its foothills which grow lower as they approach the shore and whose ridges, crowned with pines and covered with pasturage, form a magnificent amphitheater. Its beauty is enchanced by the verdure of the different canyons which intersect the country, presenting an admirable variety and harmony to the eye."

More thorough exploration, a few years later, gives further details of what they saw. Much of the country around the Golden Gate was forested with laurel, ash, oaks, live oaks, and redwoods—full of bears, deer and elk—with some stretches of sand, marsh or green flats near the shore. Whales were spouting. Sea otter, with priceless pelts, and sea lions played among the rocks. Far down San Francisco Bay stood the tall redwood tree from which modern Palo Alto takes its name. As redwoods go, it was not a very tall tree—a mere 140 or 150 feet; but it stood out so clearly, "rising like a great tower," that two Spanish parties paused to measure it. The tree still stands, having in the intervening 175 years grown only a few more feet.

The beach of San Francisco Bay was "not clean, but muddy, miry and full of sloughs," while San Pablo Bay, to the north, seemed to have cleaner beaches. The tableland where today the Presidio stands was "very green and flower-covered, with an abundance of violets." Looking out from this, a missionary priest reflected: "If it could be well settled like Europe there would not be any thing more beautiful in all the world, for it has the best advantages for founding in it a most beautiful city."

The Oakland side of the bay was a mingling of open country, forest, and small pools, with small Indian villages. It had a thick growth of iris and other plants with edible roots, and was just as full of bears as the western shore, with occasional large herds of elk.

Pushing north around San Francisco Bay, the Spanish explorers came, on October 10, 1769, to their first sight of one of the great wonders of the western world—"some tall trees of reddish-colored wood of a species unknown to us, having leaves very unlike those of the Cedar, and without a cedar odor; and as we knew not the names of the trees, we gave them that of the color of the wood, *palo colorado*" —and so now, in the twentieth century, they are "redwoods."

They were an astonishing spectacle. Sailors looking landward had noticed tall timber; but, from a mile or two offshore, an extra hundred feet or so makes very little difference, so that no one had any idea how very big the big trees were. For the first time, white men realized their hugeness. A later Spanish explorer, passing a thick grove of redwoods below San Francisco, near Watsonville (where there are none today), amused his comrades by riding his horse into a cavity in one of them, exclaiming: "Now I have a house in case it rains."

Some miles north of San Francisco, Portolá and his men began to find landmarks which, though they had never seen them, they could recognize from mariners' descriptions. They saw the white cliffs and sands about Point Reyes and Drake's Bay. Now they realized they had missed Monterey Bay entirely, and were far north of the place they had set out to find. On their way back to San Diego, they paused to erect a cross on its very shores, and still did not recognize it as Monterey Bay.

Their blunder was not so great as it seems. Finding the bay from the sea was one thing; finding it from the shore side in that luxuriant primitive wilderness was quite another. Besides, they had expected a protected harbor, not an open bay. Safely back in San Diego January 24, 1770, Portolá set out again for Monterey a few months later. By the month of May, he was safely camped there, and admiring its beauty and vegetation, with reeds and grass so tall that in some places they "would entirely cover a man on horseback, proof of the fertility of the soil." Portolá built a fort and prepared to defend California "from the atrocities of the Russians."

Other Spanish exploration swiftly followed and missions began to develop in California. Though Spaniards had sailed along the coasts of Oregon, Washington, and Canada, they had done little more. In the meantime, Russian explorers, working separately, Vitus Bering and Alexei Cherikov, had reached the northern coast of North America by 1741. The former may have come down along upper California's coast. Bering died on his second voyage, but his crew returned with one thousand otter skins and news of the creatures' breeding grounds, which started a wild craze for the fur trade.

Though the forests of the Pacific coast provided furs of almost every kind, the great prize was the sea otter, found nowhere else in the world. Herds of several hundred at a time splashed about from Kamchatka to Alaska, and all the way down the American coast to Lower California. The animals were about four and a half feet long, with a loosely folded skin that traders could stretch to a full six feet. They haunted the thick beds of kelp, near reefs and rocky islands. The Pacific kelp formed a kind of submarine jungle, in which the animals were safe from their only enemies—sea lions, sharks, and killer whales.

The explorers thought the otters most engaging creatures. They were playful, juggling bits of seaweed as they lay on their backs in the water, or playing with their pups, which paddled about in the water with their mothers. One sailor wrote: "Nothing can be more beautiful than one of these animals when seen swimming, especially when on the lookout for some object. At such times it raises its head quite above the surface, and the contrast between the shining black and the white, together with the sharp ears and a long tuft of hair rising from the middle of its forehead, which look like three small horns, render it quite a novel and attractive object."

The pelt was jet black except for white markings on the head, an exquisite, thick, soft fur, making a perfect accompaniment to the silk garments of the luxury-loving Chinese upper classes. The fine, close fur of the stubby tail was an especially valuable bit, often sold separately. As early as 1750, the Russians were taking so many furs into China that other nations woke to the opportunity.

Relentless hunting eventually practically exterminated the animals. Protected now by international treaty (1911), the almost extinct species have begun to increase again. In 1938 a small herd, the first in a hundred years, appeared at Carmel, California, where they have been ever since. It is believed that there are now over twelve thousand. Like the buffalo, the sea otter is now probably safe from extinction.

But at the end of the eighteenth century, the possible extinction of a beautiful and interesting species troubled the Pacific traders not a whit. They simply rushed in where there was a chance for profits, and the profits were enormous. A single cargo might be worth a million dollars. One guileless Indian tribe traded $8,000 worth of furs for an old chisel. It was iron! White traders soon discovered that the red man's eagerness for chisels and blue beads could give the traders a wonderful advantage in fur business.

Governments began to take an interest in country like this. England had a vague claim to New Albion, based on Drake's original discovery. While the American Revolution was still being fought out, Captain James Cook, with two ships, set out for a journey around the world, which was to include the west coast of the United States.

In the spring of 1778 he was sailing along the coast of Oregon and Washington. Cook and his men found Indians so eager for brass that they stripped all the buttons off their clothes in exchange for otter pelts. Copper kettles, tin canisters, candlesticks, and any metal they could spare went for furs. Later, when they came to the Orient, they sold the skins at a high price.

News of the small fortunes that Cook's men had made in the Chinese fur trade spread quickly. About 1792, a group of Boston merchants, scenting profits, sent out two vessels. One of these was the *Columbia* which eventually, under the Rhode-Island-born Captain Robert Gray, discovered the Columbia River. At about the same time another British expedition under Captain George Vancouver set out for a voyage around the world, which was to include further exploration of America's west coast.

When Vancouver was looking at the coastal area lying west of the future site of Portland—"a most luxuriant landscape"—he noticed that the sea had "river colored water." But the shore had the appearance of a continuous forest, and there was no harbor, the sandy beach sloping under shallow water three and four miles to sea.

On April 29, 1792, he met by chance the ship *Columbia,* nineteen months out of Boston, commanded by Captain Robert Gray. From him Vancouver learned to his disgust that the "river colored water" came from the mighty Columbia, which he had himself just missed and which Gray had discovered and explored.

Gray's discovery of the Columbia was due to his grim persistence. Where others had suspected the presence of a great river, looked for it a little while, and then sailed on, Gray stubbornly stayed. For nine days a powerful current, whose source he could not see, held his ship off the coast. It was clear that the current must come from a river somewhere, out of sight. Then a favorable wind came at last, strong enough to enable him to force the *Columbia* into the great estuary, and up the river itself on May 12, 1792.

When Vancouver learned of the Yankee achievement, he sent Lieutenant Broughton, commanding the little H.M.S. *Chatham,* 119 miles upstream, using a rough chart which Gray had supplied.

It was such a landscape as none of the discoverers had ever seen. Beyond the estuary, the Clatsop Plains were deep with grass and bright with flowers most of the year. In May, when the newcomers saw them, they were at their best. Off the shore were whales, seals, herds of sea otter by the hundreds. On the shore were clams—so many that the shell mounds left by hungry Indians still occupy many acres. Within the river's mouth the banks were "covered with forest of the very finest pine timber, fir, and spruce, interspersed with Indian settlements. Unlike Atlantic coastal forests, these were crowded with underbrush and the ground was often swampy, so that hunters sometimes found it impossible to penetrate at all. Lewis and Clark, coming this way in a few years' time, describe bogs that would shake for half an acre around, from the weight of just one man. Some hunters found the forests terrifying—"their deep and impervious gloom resembles the silence and solitude of death."

The banks of the Columbia had none of the monotony of so many wooded rivers, as its forests alternated with green open meadows.

Up the river in the spring came the salmon, ascending into Rocky Mountain streams to spawn. Bears stood by the riverside, flipping the great salmon out with their huge paws. There were so many bears that the Indians set deadfalls, baited with fish, along the river banks. Seals and sea otter came far inland up the stream. Wild ducks, geese, and cranes haunted the river as well as the coast. At times flocks of geese were so big that their passage overhead cut off the light like the drawing of a curtain.

Since seamen never went much more than a hundred miles up the Columbia, they missed much of its finest scenery, which was first described by the Lewis and Clark *Journals*. Broughton's men only heard that there were rapids upstream. They never saw the splendid pictures of the Long and Short Narrows, the Cascades and the Dalles pouring between wild shores. Lewis and Clark were the first to describe the towering rock precipices, the delicate lace of waterfalls tumbling a sheer hundred feet or more; towers, castles, and pinnacles in the colored rock.

Now, in the late autumn of 1805, from the mouth of the Clearwater, near Lewiston, Idaho, where the Lewis and Clark Corps of Discovery had camped to rest up from their exhausting climb over the Rockies, these travel-worn adventurers floated down the Columbia, being the first white men to see the river, above the point to which Lieutenant Broughton had ascended thirteen years before.

It was a wild canoe journey, with many wrecks, though none of them was fatal. The great snow-crowned peaks of Mount Adams, Mount St. Helens, Mount Hood, and the rest, loomed up at huge distances when the weather was fair, vanished into the mists for days at a time when Oregon winter rains set in. At the Short Narrows, the whole tremendous stream was compressed between rock walls only forty-five yards apart, but the expedition shot down the swift water in their canoes, "notwithstanding the horrid appearance of this agitated gut swelling, boiling & whorling in every direction." Beyond this the river boiled between walls of black rock and, at the Cascades, where the river dropped sixty feet in two miles, not even these daring canoemen risked the passage. They portaged around it, and were soon discoverers no longer, for they were floating down the lower river where white men had already journeyed.

As Lewis and Clark approached the sea, the wind grew more violent, the waves higher, the water first brackish and then salt. Eventually it became so salty that men fell ill from using it to prepare the dried and pounded fish which was now their miserable diet.

The weather was foggy, cold, and raw. Their bedding was rotting away. Their leather clothing, perpetually wet, was rotting, too, and there was no way to replace it. Game was scarce and there was no time to tan hides even if they had them.

The shores were steep and rocky, with picturesque pinnacles here and there. But though the scenery was awesome and magnificent, there was no place to camp. Steep hills came so close to the shore that there was no level ground to lie on. Their baggage had to be piled on a tangle of poles to keep it above the tide, when they went into camp on the night of November 8-9, in what is now Gray's Bay. It was one of the worst camp sites that even the Corps of Discovery had ever known in all their weary journey.

Everyone was wet. One of the canoes sank before it could be unloaded. The others filled and sank during the night. It was all the party could do to save their dugouts from complete destruction, for the tide brought in immense trees, two hundred feet long, four to seven feet through, dashing them against the beach. It was an unpleasant way to discover the size of the famous Oregon timber.

But very soon there was full compensation for all this when the day came on which Clark could write in his journal:

"Ocean in view! O! the joy."

Epilogue

FTER four hundred years, there was little left for discoverers to seek in North America. Now, white men have seen it all. With a few years of the second half of the twentieth century already past, the continent has changed so much that the first explorers would not recognize it for the land they found.

The great forests that swept across the United States, unbroken from the Atlantic coast to the Great Plains, are gone, leaving only here and there a few tracts of virgin timber, preserved by some fortunate accident. Most of Canada, too, has been lumbered over, once at least. In the wilder parts of the continent, second growth timber has come back, re-creating mighty woodlands, which though smaller than the great woods of ancient days, give some faint likeness of the forested glory of primitive America. Sometimes, for an instant, grazing cattle—black, distant dots on the prairie—suggest the wandering herds of buffalo; but the hard-riding, war-bonneted Sioux will never again, except in moving-pictures, sweep up over the prairie hillocks and ride hell-for-leather upon the casual traveler.

There are some things that not even the destructive white man can change. The Rockies and the Sierras tower to the sky, now as always, changeless. Staunch conservationists have saved a few magnificent remnants of the redwood forests. A few of the great trees still grow, as they have been growing through the whole of the Christian era. Rolling Dakota grasslands are often much the same as the prairies where the Sioux roamed in ancient days. The Painted Desert, except for a few automobile roads and transitory buildings is what it always was.

The Grand Canyon is another of the magnificent spectacles that nothing will ever change. Only twice have white men traversed the whole length of its roaring, foaming river and lived to tell the tale. In the changeless Canyon, the Havasupai still live a life almost like that of primitive days. The Indian has not gone from his ancient hunting grounds by any means. Here and there—in pueblos, in the mountains, in some Canadian forests, even in New York State—the ancient red man's faiths still live, the voices of the spirits still speak, the rites of immemorial ages still are practiced, for there is a stubborn conservatism about the red man. There are red hunters and red trappers still, roving North America's woods, living almost the life of primitive times. But, for the most part, the Indian is on his reservation or is embracing the citizenship of a country that belongs to him, at least as much as it can ever belong to any white man. He enters the white man's life.

Even the animals the red men hunted are still about. The red fox lurks within a hundred miles of New York City. Hawks and sometimes eagles soar near New England factories. In parts of North America there are more deer than when the white men came, and their old enemies, the wolf and cougar, are not extinct, though constantly hunted. But with white habitation ever spreading, the wild creatures will shy away.

Only a few are really gone for good—the great auk, the heath hen, the passenger pigeon, perhaps the Carolina parroquet and the ivory-billed woodpecker. The buffalo and sea otter, once on the verge of extinction, have been saved.

Changed though it is, the land that the first explorers found slowly through the arduous years, still remains implicit with adventure, facing new perils where peril always was, but also finding new achievement where achievement never ceased. One wonders what those first travelers—in ships, longboats, keelboats, pirogues, canoes, on foot and horseback and in the prairie schooners, wandering the forests, piercing the canebrakes, riding the prairies, scrambling dangerously in desolate mountain passes, wet, cold, sun-scorched and hungry, hunted, ever in danger of their lives—might think could they see today the land they were the first to see.

INDEX